THE ARBITRARY INDIAN

THE ARBITRARY INDIAN

The Indian Arts and Crafts Act of 1990

Gail K. Sheffield

UNIVERSITY OF OKLAHOMA PRESS
Norman and London

This publication is designed to provide accurate information in regard to the subject matter covered. It is sold with the understanding that neither the publisher nor the author is engaged in rendering legal, accounting, or other professional services. If legal advice or other expert assistance is required, the services of a competent professional person should be sought.

Library of Congress Cataloging-in-Publication Data

Sheffield, Gail K., 1940–
The arbitrary Indian: the Indian Arts and Crafts Act of 1990 /
Gail K. Sheffield.
p. cm.
Includes bibliographical references and index.
ISBN 0-8061-2969-7 (cloth: alk. paper)
1. Indian arts—Law and legislation. 2. Indian handicraft industries—Law and legislation. 3. Indians of North America—Legal status, laws, etc. 4. Art—Forgeries—United States. I. Title
KF8210.A57S53 1997
344.73'097'08997—dc21 97-9593
CIP

Text design by Cathy Carney Imboden. Text is set in Weiss.

The paper in this book meets the guidelines for permanence and durability of the Committee on Production Guidelines for Book Longevity of the Council on Library Resources, Inc. ∞

1 2 3 4 5 6 7 8 9 10

CONTENTS

PREFACE

Several years ago, I discovered the fascinating world of federal Indian law. As both a lawyer and an anthropologist, I firmly believe that law and anthropology have much to offer each other; indeed, it is probably not coincidental that several of the founders of anthropology as a discipline were lawyers. Federal Indian law is unique in the United States because it recognizes and enhances the political separation of American Indians from the remainder of American society, thus presenting opportunities for anthropologists interested in studying the inevitable social and cultural implications.

When I first read the Indian Arts and Crafts Act of 1990, it struck me instantly as ripe for such scrutiny; my subsequent inquiry beyond its surface confirmed my initial impression. A federal statute applicable nationwide creates difficulties for research, but fortunately for the purposes of my own research this statute generated such controversy that a number of prestigious organizations brought together affected and knowledgeable American Indians from diverse backgrounds and with various points of view to discuss the issues raised. Three of the forums cited in this study took place before I began my research, but I was able to gain access to them because the proceedings of the first two were taped and those of the third transcribed. I attended the others and take the quoted comments either from tapes of the proceedings or from my personal notes. I also obtained documents from the Indian Arts and Crafts Board, a subagency of the Department of the Interior, drawing upon these and various other government documents as sources for my analysis.

In the course of my travel and research, I met many kind and interesting American Indians who spoke to me about the act. I thank them. I also wish to thank Atlatl, a Native American arts organization, and the Oklahoma State Arts Council, Archives Division, for permission to quote from their tape recordings. Because this study is based on my doctoral dissertation, I also wish to thank Professors Munro Edmonson, Victoria Bricker, and Justin Rudelson, my thesis committee at Tulane University, for their guidance. Alice Stanton, my editor, helped to prod my more awkward prose into better, not to mention more grammatically correct, form. And I am grateful to my husband, who helped me in ways he knows about and even more that he does not.

THE ARBITRARY INDIAN

INTRODUCTION

A problem calls for a solution. The problem: imitation American Indian arts and crafts imported into the United States from countries such as Mexico, the Philippines, and China, and sold by unscrupulous dealers as genuine (U.S.) Indian-made goods. A lesser, but related, problem is the misrepresentation by some American artists who questionably claim Indian descent and heritage. There is, however, some disagreement concerning the criteria by which one can claim legitimate American Indian identity. The solution, according to Congress: pass a law making it illegal to sell or offer for sale goods falsely identified as Indian-made. Such legislation is intended to help American Indian artists and craftspeople economically, protect the industry from erosion of consumer confidence, and protect the unwary buyer. However, as I will demonstrate, even seemingly benign legislation concerning American Indians often strikes at the very core of their existence. This is not an original observation; much of the legislation of the past that proved so devastating to tribalism and cultural integrity was enacted to "help" American Indians. Such help generally meant promoting (or forcing) their assimilation into the dominant white society. Since the 1960s, however, federal policy has sought to encourage self-determination. The Indian Arts and Crafts Act of 1990 (Pub. L. 101-644, amending 25 U.S.C. § 305 and 18 U.S.C. §§ 1158 and 1159) was enacted in that context.

Law in modern multicultural societies often addresses ethnic concerns, thus requiring implicit or explicit definitions of ethnic groups. This study will examine what went into—and came out of—the process of defining "Indian" and "Indian tribe" for the purposes of the 1990 federal statute. The purpose of the study is to discover, through the controversy raised in the Indian arts and crafts community, the dissonances that can (and perhaps usually do) arise with the drafting of legislative definitions in furtherance of the purposes of a specific statute. Whereas the statute speaks to an ethnic activity—the self-identification of an artist in the promotion and sale of his or her work—enrollment in a tribe is a political act or status, although it may be simultaneously an ethnic act as well.

Legal definitions of ethnic groups and individuals determine who is included in and excluded from the applicable provisions. Even the most cleverly drawn definition will not conform exactly to social reality in a world of fluid social and ethnic boundaries. But, for legal purposes, it is enough if the definition is reasonably workable. "Indian" and "Indian tribe" and related terms have served the purpose of federal law in the United States for some time, although their meanings vary according to the purposes for which they are involved and the legal context in which they arise (Cohen 1982: 3). Definitions of Indians and Indian tribes in federal Indian law are *political*; they determine which groups are considered to be in a quasi-sovereign relationship with the U.S. government and which individuals are eligible for various governmental programs. Those tribes with a government-to-government relationship are called "federally recognized" or "federally acknowledged"; "acknowledgment" and "recognition" are used interchangeably. Their members are usually referred to as "enrolled," but because the tribes are sovereign political entities, their members are citizens as well as members. Just as Americans are citizens of multiple polities, that is, of their cities, states, and of the United States, so are tribal members citizens of their tribe as a political sovereign entity, of their states, and of the United States. There are also other tribes that have no sovereign status and some tribes that are only recognized by their state governments (further discussed in chapter 3).

The political nature of tribal status is one step removed from considerations of "ethnicity"; reapply the political definitions to a sphere such as art and they are two steps removed, an arbitrary process that creates arbitrary effects. Pub. L. 101-644 is not ostensibly about political relationships, but about who can legally sell his or her arts or crafts as "Indian-produced." The abundant research that followed Fredrik Barth's (1969) call to look at ethnic boundaries demonstrated the great complexity of concepts such as "ethnic group," "ethnicity," and "ethnic identity," even without the complicating factor of coercive law (McCready 1983; Royce 1982; Roosens 1989).

Legal anthropology has moved beyond its focus on dispute-management (popular in the 1960s and 1970s) to a quest for an "understanding of legal processes . . . based on a broader vision" that addresses "the importance of power relationships and historical contextualization in understanding legal and social change" (Starr and Collier 1989: 3–5). Jane Collier predicts that the "current revival of interest in the study of ethnic relations" brought about by the rise in nationalism worldwide will affect legal anthropology, concurrent with a "theoretical shift" that examines the "current political and economic processes that stimulate groups to emphasize their ethnic distinctions." Although nationalism has taken on a particularly nasty connotation in the contemporary world, nevertheless, the Indian Arts and Crafts Act, because it deals with matters of tribal sovereignty and separatism, addresses concerns with nationalistic, ethnic, and power aspects. I argue that this new (and as yet unenforced) legislation is significantly different from other Indian legislation in the degree of its confusion of political with nonpolitical matters.

Pub. L. 101-644 is also of interest because at all stages it reflects and was advanced largely by American Indian interests, at least that segment involved in the arts and crafts industry. "Ethnic law" has been portrayed generally in terms of imposition by a dominant group on a subordinate one (Burman and Harrell-Bond 1979; Starr and Collier 1989). But scholars have subsequently recognized the interactive nature of the many groups or "interests" involved.

Law, say legal anthropologists Starr and Collier, is "a 'thing' constructed by human agency that is advantageous to some at the expense of others" (1989: 3). It follows that legislation is a deliberate attempt to benefit some at the expense of others, with consequences both intended and unforeseen. Law not only *is* power, it can create or change existing power relationships. Pub. L. 101-644 creates several such power shifts.

I begin with the assumption that any law, statutory or otherwise, that defines an ethnic group will have social implications beyond the narrow focus of the law, at least in the United States. Federal Indian law, which is based on the political (and often geographical) separation of certain American Indian tribes from the rest of American society, is assumed to have an even greater potential for social impact. Indian law calls out for anthropological treatment—not because it deals with American Indians, but because it exists solely to maintain and enhance (and sometimes destroy) their social and political existence as peoples separate from the dominant society of the United States. It follows that all law within this unique field carries sociocultural implications of interest to anthropologists.

The scope of this study is the Indian Arts and Crafts Act of 1990: its historical context, legislative history, and present centrality to the ongoing controversy. That controversy is the unit of analysis. The forcing of legislatively defined ethnicity against the various concepts of those affected will create the tensions that will surface in the litigation to come. Discovering the parameters of the public debate should identify the broad range of interests affected by the Indian Arts and Crafts Act of 1990. As will be expressed by the "informants" cited within, more than the protection of livelihood is at stake here. Those who have spoken publicly express a variety of concerns, including ethnic identity, survival of traditional arts and crafts, survival of Indian culture in general, protection of religious and spiritual integrity, protection of sovereignty interests, and freedom of expression. All of these concerns are interrelated with the purposes and language of the bill and the statute as enacted.

Most of the primary data presented in this study were obtained from oral and written statements made in various settings where the participants were convened expressly to discuss the statute. These forums were all (except one) national in scope and were sponsored by prestigious organizations that were able to attract highly qualified participants. Furthermore, each forum consisted of participants chosen to reflect a broad range of views. In chronological order, these forums are:

1. The congressional hearing on the original bill (HR 2006), sponsored by the U.S. House of Representatives, Committee on Interior and Insular Affairs, held in Santa Fe, New Mexico, on August 17, 1989;
2. A public forum on the Indian Arts and Crafts Act of 1990, sponsored by the State Arts Council of Oklahoma, held in Oklahoma City, Oklahoma, January 15, 1991;
3. A panel discussion (partial), Sovereignty Symposium IV, sponsored by the Oklahoma Supreme Court, Oklahoma Indian Affairs Commission, and The Sovereignty Symposium, Inc., held in Oklahoma City, June 10–12, 1991;
4. A panel discussion, biennial conference, Atlatl,[1] a Native American Arts Service Association, held in Minneapolis, Minnesota, October 24, 1992;
5. A meeting sponsored by the Thomas Jefferson Center for the Protection of Free Expression, held in the United States Capitol Building, Washington D.C., June 22, 1993;
6. Letters and written statements on file with the Indian Arts and Crafts Board, United States Department of the Interior, Washington D.C.

The participants in these forums and conferences were chosen from different backgrounds, represented different regional and tribal affiliations, spoke from a variety of professional and occupational perspectives, and professed a wide range of opinions on the potential effects of the law. There was considerable give-and-take among the chosen participants, as well as active audience participation. I believe that the quality and nature of these forums and their different emphases (legal, artistic, and political) insure a reliable and broad-based overview of the issues so far raised by the act and as expressed by those in the Indian arts and crafts industry who will be affected. I suggest that they are representative, although not in a quantitative sense, of the perspectives brought to bear on Pub. L. 101-644. Participants on the record number in excess of fifty individuals. Not all, by any means, are quoted; some are quoted more than once, and a few appeared at more than one conference (one individual is quoted in several different guises). I quoted those comments that I believe best reflect, in a balanced manner, the entire range of perspectives, not only of the participants, but also of others with whom I personally spoke.

I have endeavored to let these informants speak in their own voices to the fullest extent practicable, both to minimize projective interpretation and because they make their points eloquently. Their spoken and written comments show the potential of this statute to change social and power relationships.

Additional primary data were obtained from various government documents, such as transcripts of congressional hearings on related matters, and from speeches to Congress. Data concerning the state-recognized tribes, except where otherwise cited, were obtained through personal correspondence with the Indian Commission or governor's office in each state.

The Indian Arts and Crafts Act has important provisions other than the one of Indian identity and identification, but this study will not address them. Nor will it address the very real concerns of art dealers, gallery owners, and museum directors, who are responsible for ensuring that the art they offer for sale is Indian-made. Although they are on the front lines in the matters dealing with the sales of arts and crafts and they are subject to the penalties of the law, their problems are, nonetheless, essentially of a business and/or professional nature.

I will analyze the statute using the spoken and written responses of those affected to demonstrate the potential of this law to change social and power relationships. I will demonstrate that the Indian Arts and Crafts Act of 1990 is socially flawed because of its definitions of "Indian" and "Indian tribe." I will also argue that Pub. L. 101-644 is an example of how well-intentioned and benign legislation can be a threat to the very interests it seeks to protect, and that such danger reveals itself through an analysis of the social and political context.

Although the Indian Arts and Crafts Act was enacted in 1990, enforcement has been suspended awaiting promulgation of the administrative regulations. Why write about a statute that has not yet been enforced and may well be struck down as unconstitutional (it will most assuredly be challenged), or amended, or even repealed? It is my belief that this statute, on its apparently simple face, demonstrates some of the inherent conflicts that result from the social and political context in which any law concerning American Indians today must operate. I hope that my analysis will generate awareness of the need to exercise great care in dealing with the core elements of legislation such as legally binding definitions with ethnic content. If this statute is struck down or amended or repealed, new statutes embedded within the same context will likely continue to emerge from the federal and state legislatures.

In the forthcoming chapters I discuss the following: the making of the Arts and Crafts law (chapter 1), the legal and historical context of federal Indian law (chapter 2), federal and state recognition (chapter 3), identity issues concerning American Indians (chapter 4), and some examples of tribes that will be differentially affected (chapter 5). The final section ("Conclusions") further discusses and draws conclusions from the matters previously examined.

CHAPTER 1

THE MAKING OF THE ACT

The Indian Arts and Crafts Act of 1990 was enacted by the U.S. Congress, passed by both the House of Representatives and the Senate on October 27, 1990, and signed into law by President George Bush on November 29, 1990. It amended preexisting, but never enforced, legislation (25 U.S.C. § 305 and 18 U.S.C. §§ 1158 and 1159) (see appendix A). Cosponsors were Representative, now Senator, Ben Nighthorse Campbell (Republican-Colorado), the only American Indian presently serving in Congress, and Representative, now Senator, Jon Kyl (Republican-Arizona). The act expands the powers of the Indian Arts and Crafts Board, an agency in the United States Department of the Interior (separate from the Bureau of Indian Affairs), which has been in existence since 1935. It also significantly increases criminal penalties and creates civil remedies for violations.

In addition, the act directs the Arts and Crafts Board to "promote the economic welfare of the Indian tribes and Indian individuals through the development of Indian arts and crafts and the expansion of the market for the products of Indian art and craftsmanship" (25 U.S.C. § 305a [1992]). The board is authorized to engage in activities such as market and technical research, technical and management assistance, and the making of loan recommendations, but the core of this mandate is the creation and administration of a system of trademarks and the setting of standards for their use to insure "genuineness and quality" (25 U.S.C. § 305a [1992]). The board is also empowered to refer complaints for criminal investigation and prosecution to the attorney general and (through the secretary of the interior) to sue for civil remedies on behalf of Indian individuals, tribes, and arts and crafts organizations (25 U.S.C. § 305d and e [1992]). An Indian tribe may also initiate civil proceedings on its own behalf or on behalf of an individual member or arts and crafts organization. There is no provision for an Indian individual or an arts and crafts organization to bring civil proceedings directly (25 U.S.C. § 305e [1992]).

The civil and criminal penalties prescribed by the act are formidable. The prohibited behavior for both kinds of penalties is the same: "To offer or display for sale or sell any good, with or without a Government trademark, in a manner that falsely suggests it is Indian produced, an Indian product, or the product of a particular Indian or Indian tribe or Indian arts and crafts organization, resident within the United States" (18 U.S.C. § 1159 [1992]; see also 25 U.S.C. § 305e [1992]). A first offense is punishable by up to a maximum fine of $250,000 and five years imprisonment, or $1,000,000 for a person other than an individual, such as a corporation. Subsequent offenses may bring a maximum penalty of $1,000,000 and fifteen years imprisonment or, for a nonindividual offender, a $5,000,000 fine (18 U.S.C. § 1159a and b[1]&[2] [1992]). Civil remedies include injunctive relief and "the greater of . . . treble damages" or, for each aggrieved Indian individual, tribe, or arts and crafts organization, "not less than $1,000 for each day on which the offer or display for sale or sale continues" (25 U.S.C. § 305e[a][2] [1992]). Punitive damages, costs, and attorney's fees are also authorized.

The act's definition of "Indian" is "any individual who is a member of an Indian tribe; or for the purpose of this section is certified as an Indian artisan by an Indian tribe" (25 U.S.C. § 305d [1992]; 18 U.S.C. § 1159[c][2] [1992]). An "Indian tribe" is:

> (A) any Indian tribe, band, nation, Alaska native village, or other organized group or community which is recognized as eligible for the special programs and services provided by the United States to Indians because of their status as Indians; or
> (B) any Indian group that has been formally recognized as an Indian tribe by a State legislature or by a State commission or similar organization legislatively vested with State tribal recognition authority. (25 U.S.C. § 305d[4] [1992]; 18 U.S.C. § 1159c[4] [1992])

An "Indian arts and crafts organization" is "any legally established arts and crafts marketing organization composed of members of Indian tribes" (25 U.S.C. § 305d[4] [1992]; 18 U.S.C. § 1159[c][4] [1992]). The act also prohibits the charging of a fee to certify an artisan.

The Indian Arts and Crafts Board was also charged with the responsibility of drafting the regulations to flesh out the Indian Arts and Crafts Act of 1990. The Indian Arts and Crafts Board is an agency of the Department of the Interior but is not part of the Bureau of Indian Affairs, which is also within that department. The term "board" refers both to the agency, being part of its name, and to the Board of Commissioners appointed to advise the agency staff. The members of the Board of Commissioners, being five in number, are appointed by the secretary of the Department of the

Interior and act solely in an advisory capacity, without compensation, to the staff of the Indian Arts and Crafts Board, headquartered in Washington, D.C. In addition to its activities in providing advice and assistance to individuals and organizations in the American Indian arts and crafts industry, the Indian Arts and Crafts Board operates three museums: the Southern Plains Indian Museum in Anadarko, Oklahoma; the Sioux Indian Museum in Rapid City, South Dakota; and the Museum of the Plains Indian, in Browning, Montana. It also publishes a source directory for American Indian arts enterprises and sponsors sales exhibitions in its museums.

This regulation-writing exercise by the board is of interest because it is a delegation by Congress to the executive branch, here to the Department of the Interior and its subagency, the Indian Arts and Crafts Board, under the general authority of 5 U.S.C.A. § 301 (1993) and the specific authority of 25 U.S.C.A. § 305b (1993). "There is a vast difference in what a statute *means* and how it is *interpreted* in a programmatic sense . . . in terms of program directives" carried out by the administrators (Deloria and Lytle 1984: 154). The Department of the Interior has, through the years, been given a great deal of authority in regulating Indian affairs. For example, the current federal recognition criteria and procedures, implemented in 1978, are administrative, not statutory. They were promulgated by the Department of the Interior, through the Bureau of Indian Affairs, Branch of Acknowledgment and Research, and are defined in 25 C.F.R. § 83 (1993) (see appendix C).

Enforcement of the new statute has awaited the promulgation of the final regulations. Proposed regulations drafted by the Arts and Crafts Board's staff were published on October 13, 1994 (59 FR 51908; corrected 59 FR 52588).

The final regulations were published on October 21, 1996 (61 FR 54551-54556, codified in 25 CFR part 309), with an effective date of November 20, 1996 (see appendix D). Section 309.1 states that the purpose of the regulations is to "define the nature and Indian origin of products protected by the Indian Arts and Crafts Act of 1990 . . . and specify how the Indian Arts and Crafts Board will interpret certain conduct for enforcement purposes." The definitions given in section 309.2 add to those of the statute by defining an "Indian product" as "any art or craft product made by an Indian," but excludes any made before 1935. "Handcrafts" are "objects created with the help of any such devices as allow the manual skill of the maker to condition the shape and design of each individual product." Stylistically, Indian arts and crafts include both traditional and nontraditional styles and media. Section 309.3 provides that the unqualified use of the terms "Indian," "Native American," or the use of the name of a particular tribe will be interpreted to mean that the product is an Indian product under these regulations, and that their maker is a member of, or certified as an artisan by, an Indian tribe or the named tribe, and that the tribe is resident in the United States. Products from countries other than the United States are exempted so long as the "name of the foreign country of tribal ancestry is clearly disclosed in conjunction with marketing of the product"; merely having country-of-origin marking on the product is not sufficient. Section 309.3 further states that an individual who is neither a member of, nor certified by, a tribe, may truthfully state that he or she is of Indian or American Indian descent, or of descent from a named tribe. To be certified as a nonmember artisan, the individual is required by section 309.4 to be "of Indian lineage of one or more members of such Indian tribe" and the certification must be "documented in writing by the governing body of an Indian tribe or by a certifying body delegated this function by the governing body of the Indian tribe." Section 309.6 directs that complaints about alleged violations of the act be made in writing and sent to the Indian Arts and Crafts Board.

The Indian Arts and Crafts Board was created in 1935 by the original Indian Arts and Crafts Act as part of the so-called Indian New Deal of the Roosevelt administration. The board's mission, as set forth in the 1935 act, was "to promote the economic welfare of the Indian Tribes and the Indian wards of the Government through the development of Indian arts and crafts and the expansion of the market for the products of Indian art and craftsmanship" (25 U.S.C. § 305a [1988]). To accomplish that mission, Congress gave to the board numerous powers, which were clearly of a supportive nature. They included functions such as the undertaking of market and technical research, correlating and encouraging the activities of governmental and private agencies, offering assistance in the management of operating groups, making loan recommendations, and creating government trademarks for Indian products. This was clearly a nurturing mandate. There were no civil remedies and criminal penalties were negligible. Not a single case has been prosecuted in the half century since its enactment.

Robert Fay Schrader, a chronicler of the board's early history, tells us that President Franklin Delano Roosevelt's New Deal was "particularly evident . . . in Indian affairs . . . [where] strong personalities received a mandate to carry into action programs that had been smothered for years by uninterested or inept administrators" (1983: xi). The strongest personality in Indian Affairs was Commissioner John Collier of the Indian Office, who was largely responsible for the

Indian Reorganization Act of 1934 (see chapter 2). According to Schrader, this era was characterized by "an unselfish devotion to a new set of ideals on the part of individuals working in and with the Indian Office between 1935 and 1945. Preservation rather than destruction of Indian life became the guiding principle behind the official policy" (xi–xii).

Schrader describes in depth the accomplishments of the Indian Arts and Crafts Board during its florescence in its first decade of existence (1983). He explains how the late nineteenth century American interest in arts and crafts created a demand for American Indian crafts. Many non-Indians saw in this demand an opportunity for a coherent industry that could serve to improve Indians' lives economically, further assimilation, preserve indigenous art, and preserve a way of life.

A precursor to the New Deal reforms was the massive report commissioned by the secretary of the interior, generally referred to as the Meriam Report after the name of the technical director, Lewis Meriam (Institute for Government Research 1928). The report addressed all areas of Indian existence, including the state of handcraft production. The field investigators reported that in only a few tribes were arts and crafts of significant economic importance and that in some arts and crafts production had virtually disappeared (531). Almost all arts and crafts with commercial potential, except for silver jewelry-making in the Southwest, were made by women (532). The greatest loss of traditional arts was associated with the poorest tribes. For various reasons, such as the unavailability of suitable materials or lack of craftsmanship applied to items to be sold as curios, quality was often poor except where there was a market for high-quality goods such as Navajo silver work and the pottery of certain Pueblos. Prior government encouragement had been erratic and limited to instruction in schools rather than aimed at stimulating on-reservation production (648). The report concluded that the preservation of these potential income sources would require government aid in production and marketing, and recommended that Indian arts and crafts production be encouraged for economic, social, and psychological reasons (125, 533).

The activities of the newly created board in promoting "quality" are subject to two opposing interpretations. According to Fredrick Dockstader (1961: 29), the Meriam Report field surveyors found many craft workers still living, but not producing because of prior repressive government actions:

> By a quirk in the administrative process, it had been thought perfectly all right for Indians to turn out gewgaws and trinkets for curio shops, yet serious art efforts were completely forbidden. Older women, skilled in the arts, had ceased much of their production, and the younger girls had no training or incentive to develop skills.
>
> However, with the encouragement and interest shown by the fieldworkers, together with the removal of restrictive measures, hidden talent emerged. Older women came out of retirement to teach the younger ones, and soon it was discovered that many of the old techniques were not actually gone, as had been feared.
>
> Eventually, as a result of the Board's encouragement, demand for high standards, and assistance at crucial points, a period of peak artcraft production was reached.

One of the Atlatl conference participants, however, saw the board's activities in a less positive light. He prefaced his remarks with reference to Dockstader and the Meriam Report's recommendations that the Indian Office develop a program with the dual goals of encouraging the production of high-quality goods and developing a market for them. To meet the goal of high quality, the Meriam Report (Institute for Government Research 1928: 651) said that items should be "characteristically Indian," made of good materials, and be of good workmanship, color, and design. Additionally, they should be usable unless made for display only, unique or original, "tagged with the government's guarantee of genuineness and quality," and fairly priced (651). Furthermore, "to achieve these things, it would be necessary to exercise some supervision over the workers in their homes. Employees should see that the workers avoid mistakes that would make articles unsaleable and that they be enabled to secure the best materials to be had. It would be necessary to stimulate originality of design, to encourage regularity of production, and to require as far as possible good working conditions in the homes" (651–52). The complaining Atlatl conference participant suggested that to direct Indian arts and crafts toward a non-Indian market, under supervision and direction of persons "not . . . familiar with a particular culture . . . smacks of cultural imperialism." He further suggested that the new statutory scheme evidenced an intent by the federal government to "gain firm control over the production of Indian arts," an attitude he felt was still extant and operative through the new Indian Arts and Crafts Act.

In fairness to the Meriam Report policy makers and the early board, the early decades of the twentieth century were particularly desperate times for many native peoples, and the writers of the report were cognizant of that problem, stating that "many of [the fieldworkers] know little better than the Indians how to secure material or how to find good markets for the finished work. Neither have they the time, or in some instances the taste or the skill, to control the quality of the work done, and the difficulty of disposing of low grade products has proved the chief obstacle to the development of markets where the effort has been made" (648).

It is unclear whether the 1990 regime creates or requires a more aggressive policing role for the Indian Arts and Crafts Board, a function for which it was not designed. The act does authorize and direct the board to screen complaints and to recommend, through the secretary of the Department of the Interior, whether a case should be referred to the attorney general of the United States for criminal prosecution and/or civil proceedings. Comment on the board's proper role was voiced at the June 22, 1993, meeting in the U.S. Capitol Building (Thomas Jefferson Center 1993) by an angry and outspoken opponent of the act, an enrolled member of a western tribe. This artist-craftsman argued that the original intent of the 1935 statute was to provide employment and promote the marketing of arts and crafts, but that the amended statute only protects the consumer. He further suggested that the amended statute, in addition to being divisive and unworkable, is just another federal law that has been, and will continue to be, detrimental to Indian peoples, and that the federal legislation serves only to control Indian peoples and perpetuate colonialism.

As noted above, the major rationale for the enactment in 1990 of Pub. L. 101-644 was the ongoing and constantly increasing impact in the American Indian arts and crafts industry of imitation Indian arts and crafts being fraudulently sold as genuine. This continues to be a difficult problem; because the act has not been enforced prior to the November 20, 1996, effective date of the regulations, its problem-solving capacity is still untried. Misrepresentation is not a new problem, as evidenced by the passage of the 1935 act. In 1985, the United States Department of Commerce, at the request of Congress, prepared a report entitled "Study of Problems and Possible Remedies Concerning Imported Native American-Style Jewelry and Handicrafts" (U.S. Department of Commerce 1985). It addresses only the problem of imported imitation Indian jewelry and goods, not the domestic impersonator problem. Not only has the quantity of imported goods been increasing, but the quality has become more sophisticated, thus making detection of counterfeits more difficult. Indeed, "entrepreneurs send supplies and samples to foreign countries, where an experienced and inexpensive work force duplicates the original sample . . . sometimes even [reproducing] the craftsman's signature" (4).

Although many types of handcrafts are imitated, the major economic threat comes from the sale of imitation Southwest Indian jewelry (4). Most of these imports are channeled through the markets in Denver, Albuquerque, and Phoenix (5). The threat is multi-faceted—loss of income to American Indian producers due to the cheaper prices of the imitation imported goods; a loss of confidence in the market by buyers who are uncertain of the authenticity of the jewelry offered; and less obvious, but no less important, types of damage as suggested by those who have spoken out about their concerns with issues affecting sovereignty and cultural integrity.

The economic impact is considerable. The Commerce Department report estimated that unmarked imports siphon off 10–20% of the total estimated *annual* industry value of 400–800 million dollars. That means 40–80 million dollars in *annual* losses, sustained primarily by the Zuni, Navajo, and Hopi, who dominate the jewelry market (4). Those estimates were made in 1985; presumably the figures have grown in the intervening decade. Other quality goods subject to this fraudulent activity include beadwork made by members of Plains tribes in the Dakotas and Oklahoma, paintings, rugs, sandpaintings, pottery, baskets, katcina dolls,[1] and religious objects (3).

The absurd aspect of this problem is that, according to this government report, the Tariff Act of 1930 (19 U.S.C.A. § 1304[a]) *requires* imported products to be labeled with their country of origin:

> Every article of foreign origin . . . shall be marked in a conspicuous place as legibly, indelibly, and permanently as the nature of the article (or container) will permit in such a manner as to indicate to an ultimate purchaser in the United States the English name of the country of origin of the article. (U.S. Department of Commerce 1985: 6)

The report noted that comments obtained from craftspeople, manufacturers, wholesalers, and retailers in the Indian arts and crafts industry suggested that the best solution was to require such permanent markings (3). Despite this statutory requirement of permanent country-of-origin marking for all imported goods, the Commerce Department reported that:

> present U.S. Customs Service regulations allow gummed, stick-on labels to be used on jewelry and crafts. Consequently, industry representatives allege that some jewelry and craft dealers and wholesalers remove the labels from the imported goods and sell the products as authentic Native American. These unmarked goods are alleged to have been sold not only in the Southwest but throughout the United States and even exported to other countries. (1985: 1)

In 1988, Congressmen Campbell and Bill Richardson (Democrat-New Mexico) sponsored an amendment (Pub. L.

100–418) to the Omnibus Trade Act that directed the United States Customs Service to write regulations for permanent markings on imported American Indian–style goods. According to Congressman Campbell, speaking at the 1989 hearing in Santa Fe, the amendment had not yet been enforced because "when the Customs Department . . . appeared at hearings on how to implement the bill, the National Jewelers Association and several other groups were opposed to it, feeling that it would hurt the whole jewelry industry in the United States, since many of our major chains are now in foreign ownership, and in fact much of the money that is coming into the United States to expand the jewelry business is foreign money" (U.S. House 1989a: 16). The Customs Service regulations subsequently written, as required by the amendment to the Omnibus Trade Act (19 C.F.R. § 134), became effective shortly before the enactment of the Indian Arts and Crafts Act in 1990 and were limited to American Indian–style goods. Perhaps that limitation will pacify the fine jewelry industry since it does not apply to other types and styles of jewelry of foreign origin. In a 1993 article, author Jon Keith Parsley suggested that the permanent marking provisions have not had time to work, and that they could probably solve the problems for which the Indian Arts and Crafts Act was created.

Another significant impetus behind the perceived need for a federal statute was the proliferation of state statutes being created to deal with the problem of fraud. These statutes truly created a patchwork of rules for Indian artists and craftspeople, and, unlike many business activities, the sale of arts and crafts is most assuredly not confined to the local scene. Congressman Campbell stated at the hearing in Santa Fe that "the time is ripe to address from a national standpoint this type of legislation . . . so that we do not end up with 50 different States having 50 different definitions of Indian art" (U.S. House 1989a: 2). Later in the hearing he said that an "emotional and angry" discussion in the New Mexico State Legislature had made him aware of the need for legislation on the federal level, and that he and Congressman Kyl had sought a "common denominator nationwide" to protect groups and individuals who "don't identify that strongly with a tribe" (153).

According to one forum participant (Atlatl), the genesis of the act grew out of the 1970s fashion craze for American Indian style, which stimulated the production of misrepresented goods. Senator Kyl's father, a former congressman and at that time assistant secretary of the interior, and an ardent admirer of Indian art, met in 1974 with representatives of the many interests involved and pledged to push the Department of the Interior toward proposing remedial legislation. This initiative ceased, however, upon the election of a new president in 1976, and the idea lay dormant until the election to the House of Representatives in 1986 of the younger Kyl. Kyl, who, as representative, had a large Navajo constituency, began the process again and, with Representative Campbell, introduced H.R. 2006 in 1989 (Atlatl 1992).

The legislation was introduced by congressmen from Arizona and Colorado, and the only hearing was held in Santa Fe, New Mexico, where the House Committee on Interior and Insular Affairs was represented only by the two cosponsors. The individuals who testified, individually or on behalf of tribes, were overwhelmingly residents of the Southwest. There was no mention of state-recognized tribes, which are found only in the East, and little mention of the types of problems that haunt the Five Tribes of eastern Oklahoma, especially the Cherokee, discussed more fully in chapter 5. (There was later, after enactment, a good deal of grumbling among those in the Oklahoma Indian arts industry about having been left out of the process.) There is not much on the record to indicate an exploration of interests in the art worlds of areas other than the Southwest, except, of course, for the inclusion of the state-recognized tribes during the revision of the original bill. Congressman Campbell, however, in a letter to the editor of *The Indian Trader* (1991), stated that the writing of the bill was preceded by "two years of work with Indian tribes, individual artists, consumer groups, the Justice Department, the Department of Interior, and various Indian art groups."

The federal statute does not, according to the Indian Arts and Crafts Board, preempt state statutes, thus still allowing each state to define "Indian" and "Indian tribe" for its own purposes as it wishes (U.S. Department of the Interior 1991: 5).

The first version of the 1990 statute saw light as proposed bill H.R. 2006; this was the subject of the congressional hearing held in Santa Fe, New Mexico, sponsored by the Committee on Interior and Insular Affairs of the House of Representatives (U.S. House 1989a). Over twenty individuals spoke or filed written statements; they included artists, gallery owners, and tribal officials. Area tribes officially represented were the Navajo, the Hopi, the Eight Northern Pueblos Council (composed of the Pueblos of Taos, Picuris, San Juan, Santa Clara, San Ildefonso, Pojoaque, Nambe, and Tesuque), the Yavapai-Apache, and the Jicarilla Apache. Their comments helped guide the revision process that resulted in the final version as enacted. However, the changes did not remedy the problems; they merely relocated them to new ground.

H.R. 2006 defined "Indian" simply as "any individual who is a member of an Indian tribe." An "Indian tribe" was "any

Indian tribe, band, nation, Alaska Native village, or any other organized group or community which is recognized as eligible for the special programs and services provided by the United States to Indians because of their status as Indians" (U.S. House 1989a: 11).

The original bill did not include any provisions for individuals who were not members of federally recognized tribes, and that issue was a matter of importance to many of the participants in the Santa Fe hearing. Most of those present, including the tribal representatives, recognized the need for an accomodation of some type for nonenrolled artists. The original bill also did not include the provisions making the law applicable to state-recognized tribes. That issue was not apparently raised, perhaps because of the western orientation of the congressional sponsors and the hearing participants. Had the hearing been held in the East, where the state-recognized tribes are located, the latter question might well have been raised. A number of the participants, not enrolled in any tribe, and each with a different kind of a claim to "Indianness," spoke at the Santa Fe hearing about their personal experiences. Some examples are as follows:

Artist Carol S. was born and reared on her father's reservation; he is an enrolled Seneca and her mother is non-Indian.

> Among my father's people, enrollment numbers are assigned through blood descent in the mother's line. In some tribes, such as the Onondaga, which is another Iroquois tribe, numbers come through the father's line. So if a person has a Seneca father and an Onondaga mother, it is not possible to get an enrollment number, even though that person is 100 percent Indian.
>
> I do not question the rights of the tribes to set whatever criteria they want for enrollment eligibility; but in my view,

> that is the extent of their rights, to say who is an enrolled Seneca or Mohawk or Navajo or Cheyenne or any other tribe. Since there are mixed bloods with enrollment numbers and some of those with very small percentages of genetic Indian ancestry, I don't feel they have the right to say to those of us without enrollment numbers that we are not of Indian heritage, only that we are not enrolled.
>
> . . . To say that I am not [Indian] and to prosecute me for telling people of my Indian heritage is to deny me some of my civil liberties, to disenfranchise me and others like me and constitutes racial discrimination.
>
> . . . What I ask is for justice for those of us who are in fact of Indian heritage by blood ancestry, whether or not we are enrolled members of Indian tribes. (U.S. House 1989a: 24–26)

Pueblo potter Margarete B., who is of three-sixteenth Indian ancestry and was raised on the reservation by her mother, a well-known Indian artist, and her full-blood grandmother, spoke as follows:

> I knew of no other lifestyle than that which was provided to me with my tribal surroundings. I learned to crawl on Navajo rugs and I ate Indian food as a part of my normal diet. I learned the smell of fresh-baked yeast bread coming out of the adobe horno and I also learned the smell of black pottery fire and manure. I knew no other way of life than what my mother and grandmother could provide. . . . I am not eligible to be enrolled with the tribe that I have been a part of, that I have been at sacred ceremonies with, that I have laughed with and cried with. Is it fair to say you can knead the dough and bake the bread because you happen to be three-sixteenth Indian, but you don't eat it because you aren't enrolled and you don't have a census number? . . . Numbers are a way of measuring people. Can numbers measure the soul? (U.S. House 1989a: 40)

Artist John N., who claims to be the grandson of a Mescalero Apache man, is an internationally known artist:

> I have never in the past nor do I now advertise my art as being Indian made. . . . My paintings are the product of intuition and vision that is personal to me. I am an American artist who happens to be part Indian, and I have no desire to advertise my ethnicity for sale in the marketplace. . . . The issue arises as to what I say in personal interviews when I am asked about my cultural heritage. Naturally, I am obliged to be truthful and neither fabricate nor deny my heritage or any part of it. . . .
>
> The hairsplitting between and among Indian people that is invited by efforts to legislate Indianness is both divisive and counterproductive. (U.S. House 1989a: 48)

Sculptor Robert G. describes himself as "multi-ethnic," with Apache ancestry on his father's side:

> I am proud of this, just as I am proud of my Mexican American, Mexican Indian and Spanish ancestry. . . . I feel strongly that no one has the right to call someone "phony" when the personal and sensitive expression of art is involved. . . . It is natural for my art to reflect my heritage. At times in my career I have leaned toward my Native American side for the subject, content and promotion of my work. This was done with complete sincerity, in the spirit of my upbringing. It never occurred to me that I was not entitled to my Native American heritage just because I wasn't assigned a number. I was, and am now, creating art that is a true personal expression of myself as an artist. . . . (U.S. House 1989a: 231–32)

Kimberly Craven, an assistant to Congressman Campbell, spoke at a public forum on the statute held in the Oklahoma Senate Chambers, Oklahoma City, on January 15, 1991. She stated that the testimony from the Santa Fe hearing concerning the plight of nonenrolled individuals and the sympathetic attitude of the tribal leaders present led to a search for a more expansive definition of "Indian" beyond enrollment in a federally recognized tribe. The version as enacted was chosen after consultation with the Department of Justice to ensure constitutionality. State-recognized tribes were included at the insistence of congressmen from some of the eastern states that recognize tribes, although not, she noted, without concern about the constitutionality of these groups as being constituted by race rather than as political entities (Public Forum 1991). Making the tribes, through the certification provision, the arbiters of who is a (nonenrolled) Indian was done in accordance with *Santa Clara Pueblo v. Martinez*, 436 U.S. 49, 98 S. Ct. 1670 (1978), in which the United States Supreme Court upheld the right of a tribe to determine its own membership by holding that its sovereign nature gave it "sovereign immunity" from suit by the plaintiff seeking membership.

Jane L. Weeks, the former director of the Alabama Indian Affairs Commission, was partly instrumental in getting the state-recognized tribes included. Weeks, who is an outspoken advocate for Alabama's non–federally recognized tribes, testified on June 23, 1988, before an advisory committee on U.S. civil rights, where she characterized Alabama's Indians as its "invisible minority."

Senator Jeff Bingaman (Democrat-New Mexico) addressed the U.S. Senate on November 26, 1991, about his concerns with the legislation as it was written (Bingaman 1991). He reiterated his support of its goals and of the sovereignty concerns of the tribes. He suggested, however, that the law might unfairly and unconstitutionally impinge on the right of individuals of Indian ancestry to practice their chosen profession in the visual arts. Further, the act could, over time, harm both the sovereignty interests of tribes and the rights of individuals to earn their livelihood and to engage in free speech. He pointed out that artists of other ethnic groups are not required to prove ancestry, nor are Indians in other professions:

> It is simply not sufficient or logical to say that non-enrolled Indians can continue with their art, so long as they refrain from talking about it in connection with their heritage.
>
> . . . The act appears to create the odious spectacle of requiring American citizens to carry paper-work establishing their racial or ethnic purity before they can fully practice their chosen professions. (Bingaman 1991)

The senator also decried as an infringement of sovereign rights any attempt by the Indian Arts and Crafts Board to require uniform criteria for certification in the regulations still-to-be written by the Indian Arts and Crafts Board. Now written, the regulations require that a tribe certify only individuals "of Indian lineage of one or more members of such Indian tribe," and that such certification "must be documented in writing by the governing body of an Indian tribe or by a certifying body delegated this function by the governing body of the Indian tribe (25 CFR part 309.4). As will be shown in chapter 5, the Yankton Sioux Tribe, prior to the regulatory scheme, certified an adopted white artist. The question is: Is this adopted but nonbiologically related individual "of Indian lineage"? If not, does that infringe upon the tribe's sovereignty?

Included in the unanswered questions are concerns such as the status of deceased artists whose works were created after 1935, and the possible legal questions raised by the North American Free Trade Agreement (NAFTA). The effects of the act also will reach beyond galleries, art shows, and museums. For example, the new Denver airport is to be graced with a $200,000 art project called "Tribute to American Indians"; the artists chosen are all to be enrolled members of federally recognized tribes indigenous to Colorado. Those left out allege discrimination; one artist is quoted as saying that "it's wrong for a publicly funded art project to be limited to artists who can prove they are members of certain tribes . . . it's un-American to show papers" (Rosen 1993). Another example:

> The top official responsible for implementing these laws, Interior Secretary Manuel Lujan, was placed in an embarrassing position last year. One of his agencies, the Bureau of Indian Affairs, gave an unusual and sizable arts and crafts contract to artist Melody L. . . . who had been excluded from the New Mexico State Fair Indian Arts Exhibition in the late 1980s under the state Indian arts misrepresentation law.
>
> The situation became even dicier when Interior's own arts and crafts shop had to cancel L. . . .'s planned exhibit because she did not meet her claimed Pueblo or Pima or even Interior's standards as an Indian. (Harjo 1991: A6)

According to his biographer, Senator Campbell said that "all in all, the bill has been acclaimed by tribes and the vast majority of Indian artists. Only a few so-called Cherokees who could not prove ancestry have complained that it is unfair" (Viola 1993: 191).

The next chapter will present the background necessary for understanding the place of American Indians in the United States political structure. Such an understanding is required to appreciate any federal Indian law.

CHAPTER 2

LEGAL CONTEXT AND SOVEREIGNTY

Two perspectives are necessary for understanding the role of law in Indian affairs. The first is the legal status of American Indians in the United States generally, which results from their relationship with the federal government and the states in which the reservations (including dependent Indian communities) are located. The second is the effect of the specific statutes, administrative regulations, and court decisions that structure Indian people's lives. Federal Indian law is pervasive; "Law dominates Indian life in a way not duplicated in other segments of American society" (Cohen 1982: vii).

Indian law evolved with and as an inherent part of the changing Indian policies in the United States and from the prior colonial milieu. It is important to note that all American Indians were unilaterally extended U.S. citizenship in 1924, which gave to them the same rights, privileges, and obligations as other American citizens were in addition to those attendant upon their special relationship with the federal government (Indian Citizenship Act of 1924, 43 Stat. 253, codified at 8 U.S.C.A. § 1401b). The unilateral bestowal of citizenship was not universally welcomed and was even politely refused by some who found it "incompatible with tribal membership in times of crisis" (Deloria 1974: 19).

"Indian law" is a term unfamiliar both to laypeople and to attorneys not involved in this specialized field. It refers to "the body of jurisprudence created by treaties, statutes, executive orders, court decisions, and administrative action defining and implementing the relationship between the United States, Indian tribes and individuals, and the states. Although tribal laws and state laws sometimes play important roles, Indian law is primarily a body of federal law" (Cohen 1982: 1).

Our blueprint for government, the U.S. Constitution, mentions Indians in only two, somewhat ambiguous, contexts. In article 1, section 8, which enumerates the powers of Congress, clause 3 empowers that body "to regulate Commerce *with* foreign nations, and *among* the several States, and *with* the Indian Tribes" (emphasis added). Read with the Treaty Clause (U.S. Const., art 2, sec. 2, cl. 2), which gives to the president, with the advice and consent of the Senate and a two-thirds vote, the power to make treaties, the Commerce Clause is considered sufficient to give Congress control over the affairs of American Indians (*Worcester v. Georgia*, 31 U.S. 515 [1832]). In 1871, however, Congress took away from the president the power to make treaties with Indians (25 U.S.C.A. § 71). Thereafter, new reservations could be created by executive order (a power remaining to the president, and one more appropriate to the postpacification period), direct congressional action, or bilateral agreements between the tribes and Congress, and, after 1978, by administrative action. Through a series of statutes enacted between 1918 and 1927, Congress withdrew from the president authority to create or change reservations by executive order (Prucha 1994: 332–33).

This unique relationship between American Indian tribes and the U.S. government is a direct result of the early British and then American decisions to deal with the Native peoples by treaty. Treaties have a lofty status; the Supremacy Clause of the U.S. Constitution provides that treaties "shall be the supreme Law of the Land" as against any contrary provisions of state law or constitutions (U.S. Const., art. 6, cl. 2).

The second direct reference in the Constitution to Indians is a reference to "Indians not taxed" in the clause concerning apportionment for congressional seats and for direct taxation (U.S. Const., art. 1, § 2, cl. 3). This clause merely excludes those noncitizen Indians who are within United States jurisdiction, but living on tribal lands (and thus not under state jurisdiction), from being counted for those purposes. The "Indians not taxed" exclusion is repeated in the Fourteenth Amendment.

The power of Congress in relation to American Indians is "plenary," but it is also limited (Cohen 1982: 217). *Black's Law Dictionary* (1968) defines "plenary" as "full, entire, complete, absolute, perfect, [and] unqualified," thus giving us the rather oxymoronic "limited plenary power." The foundation cases that describe the place of American Indian tribes in the American political system are the three early nineteenth-century "Cherokee Cases," also known as the Marshall Trilogy because all three were authored by Chief Justice John Marshall. *Johnson v. Macintosh* (21 U.S. [8 Wheat.] 543 [1823]) recognized "original Indian title," the right of occupancy by aboriginal peoples, which can be extinguished only by the federal government through purchase or conquest. *Cherokee Nation v. Georgia* (30 U.S. [5

Pet.] 1 [1831]) held that the Cherokee tribe was not a foreign state but was a distinct political society with self-government. *Worcester v. Georgia* (31 U.S. [6 Pet.] 515 [1832]), held that because the tribe was a distinct political community with its own territory, state law could not be applied. In *Cherokee Nation* and *Worcester,* Marshall characterized Indian tribes as "dependent domestic nations" with a relationship to the U.S. government that "resembles that of a ward to his guardian." Such a relationship does not strip from these nations their inherent powers of self-government because, under international law, a weak state that puts itself under the protection of a stronger power does not thereby lose its rights as a sovereign government (30 U.S. [5 Pet.] at 17; 31 U.S. [6 Pet.] at 560–61).

The emphasis added to the provisions of the Commerce Clause, above, highlights one of the legal bases on which Indian separatists claim full sovereignty. That claim interprets the Commerce Clause differently, as here summarized in the statement of the National Congress of American Indians at the 1989 congressional hearing in Santa Fe:

> The U.S. Constitution divides powers between the federal and state governments. In nationalizing dealings with Indian nations, the general government reserved powers for itself *vis à vis* the states. Neither the federal nor state governments had or have the legal authority to confer on themselves the inherent sovereign powers of Indian nations. The Constitution says that the general government deals with trade and intercourse *with* the Indian tribes, as it does *with* foreign nations, rather than as it does *among* the several states. Therefore, the conclusion should be that the federal government has plenary power *regarding,* rather than *over,* the Indian tribes, and that the Indian nations themselves are the appropriate regulators . . . in the area of tribal rights and the

establishment of remedies for the abuse of those rights. (U.S. House 1989a: 127) (emphasis in original)

The actual scope of tribal sovereignty has waxed and waned with shifts in federal policy, statutory enactments, administrative regulation and enforcement, and court decisions—all characterized by a great deal of inconsistency. The U.S. government, the various states, and the federally recognized tribes have danced through the American past, each seeking to maximize its legal position with respect to the others. To further complicate the matter, the federal government does not act as a single entity; with respect to Indian policy, it has been analogized to "a ship with three rudders, each controlled by a different helmsman" (Burton 1991: 7). The three helmsmen are Congress, the president, and the Supreme Court. This push-pull underlies virtually all of what is called "Indian law." As for the presidential helmsman, Kickingbird and Ducheneaux observe that "each administration is caught between cries for complete termination of Indian rights and solid resistance against such a move" (1973: 210).

Commentators disagree about whether there is any coherent Indian policy today. Vine Deloria, Jr., says that federal Indian policy has always been "expediency grounded only in the political considerations of the moment and without any lasting understanding of the nature of peoples, laws, governments, or responsibilities" and can be determined only by hindsight (1974: xiv; 1985: 3). Anthropologist Thomas R. McGuire argues that even though the workings of Congress, the executive branch, and the federal courts "can and do lead to capricious policy formation . . . and inconsistencies," nevertheless a set of current policy goals can be determined from an analysis of congressional and administrative policy statements and specific programs, and from federal court decisions (1990: 206). He abstracts from these sources three "concurrent goals . . . to enhance tribal sovereignty, promote economic self-sufficiency, and foster cultural self-determination," all subject to the trade-offs that result from the "realities of practicality and politics" (206, 212).

Another commentator offers the following synthesis to describe the scope of contemporary tribal sovereignty:

> The general attributes of tribal sovereignty today are: (1) Indian tribes possess inherent governmental power over all internal affairs; (2) the states are precluded from all interfering with the tribes in their self-government; and (3) Congress has plenary power to limit tribal sovereignty . . . . It may be said with accuracy that, however useful tribal sovereignty is as a source of inherent tribal power and as a shield against state intrusion, such sovereignty exists entirely at the sufferance of Congress. Political restraints may . . . keep Congress from greatly diminishing or eliminating tribal sovereignty, but legal restraints do not. (Canby 1988: 71, 79)

American Indian sovereignty in the United States today is an idea, an ideal, and a legal status. It is at the core of most, if not all, issues and problems concerning American Indian groups and their relations with the larger society. It is certainly widely misunderstood by non-Indians:

> It is difficult for the western rancher to accept that a neighboring Indian tribe has superior claims to the most precious of natural resources—water—and it is difficult for the civil libertarian to accept that a tribal government may conduct itself in some ways which would not meet the standards of due process and equal protection of the laws recognized in the United States Constitution. (Grossman 1979: iii)

The concept and scope of American Indian sovereignty today can only be understood in its historical context as it evolved from the beginning of European exploration and discovery. Although we speak of the European "discovery" of the New World, American Indians wryly ask how one can discover a land they had discovered millennia before.

It is important to understand that present-day law is built upon a foundation of judicial opinions reaching back through time. Green and Dickason tell us that the early decisions of American and Canadian courts reflected legal thinking of the time and were "in direct descent from those [legal ideas] held when the North American continent was 'discovered' and settled by Europeans" (1976: 123–25). These notions of title to territory evolved into the present day rules of international law.

Many of the earliest European "discoverers" considered the Natives of the New World merely as occupants rather than as owners of, with legal rights to, the territories that the Europeans claimed for their own sovereigns. One exception was the Dutch, who negotiated treaties from the beginning (Christian 1989: viii). Green and Dickason explain that under international law the country that first discovers and settles a new territory by that means gains title; title passes to another state through purchase or conquest (1976: 125). Settlement, however, was not a requisite for getting and keeping title in the New World. Aboriginal peoples had no legal rights of ownership and became subjects of the Crown (126). This stance also reflects policy-by-expedience inasmuch as, according to Green and Dickason, "continuous use and possession of land . . . as a basis for title dates back to Roman times . . . [as a] self-evident rule of natural law . . . recognized in Justinian's code, and continued under feudalism in common law. But it interfered with the politics of expansion, and so was circumvented during the Age of Discovery" (249). Or, as Deloria puts it, this rationalization for taking Indian lands was justified because "the white Europeans were to have the Indian lands because the Indians were infidels rather than Christians, hunters rather than farmers, monsters rather than men, or by reason of the generous gifts of European civilization and technology, or by reason of conquest, or by reason of the fact that the king owned everything" (1974: 89).

Acting quickly after Columbus's return from his first voyage to the New World, Pope Alexander VI, under his assumed authority to delegate newly discovered lands on God's earth, issued a papal bull on May 4, 1493, partitioning the new territory between Spain and Portugal (Green and Dickason 1989: 4). The emerging Protestant rulers rejected the papal distribution scheme but they did acknowledge title in other Christian rulers whose subjects had, in fact, begun settlement (4, 17). In any event, no one "thought it was necessary to secure the agreement of the local inhabitants to the assumption of sovereignty" (17). This occurred at a time when the concept of the sovereignty of nations was developing in Europe and in the process of replacing the idea of the personal sovereignty of the monarch (244).

Historical accounts of North American Indian-white legal or political relationships commonly divide the time span from 1492 until the present into periods characterized by federal policies and interrelated law. The time spans are much the same in the various accounts; I adopt here the periods defined by the U.S. Commission on Civil Rights in its 1981 report to Congress entitled *Indian Tribes: A Continuing Quest for Survival* (which begins with the year 1494).

THE COLONIAL PERIOD (1494–1776)

Unlike the Spanish pattern of colonization, which sought to utilize native labor through the feudal *encomienda* system, the British came with their families to settle. The British regarded the Native population as irrelevant, except as a source of assistance in adapting to the alien environment. In later colonial times, Indians became important to the Europeans as potential allies or enemies in their wars against each other, at which time treaty-making became useful (Grossman 1979: 3). The Doctrine of Discovery justified European assumption of title to these "unoccupied" lands, that is to say, "unoccupied by Europeans" (U.S. Commission on Civil Rights 1981: 16). As noted above, however, American Indians were recognized by the British as possessing "aboriginal title." In North America, the British kings, through their colonies, acquired real estate and other benefits, such as military alliances, through treaties with the Natives (U.S. Commission on Civil Rights 1981: 17).

THE EARLY UNITED STATES–INDIAN RELATIONS PERIOD (1776–1830)

The American Revolution replaced the Crown with the new republic, and the colonies with states. The new Americans, like the British colonists, needed the Indians as military allies and continued the practice of treaty-making. The question of federal versus state roles in dealing with the tribes had not yet been settled, and President George Washington advocated good faith dealing rather than conquest. George S. Grossman states that the first six presidents "generally pursued a policy of conciliation and peace toward Indian tribes . . . [recognizing] tribal sovereignty in treaties" (1979: 4). Even at this early time, however, the statesmen could see the future course of American expansionism. According to Grossman, "evident in their writings . . . is another theme—ominous for Indian survival—the theme that Indian tribes can be protected from the pressures of frontier expansion only for a limited time. Viewing white expansion as inevitable, even Thomas Jefferson, in a famous letter to the Cherokees, advised Indian tribes to prepare to be engulfed—advice which the Cherokees took to heart by learning the ways of Europeans, but to little avail" (4).

The Removal Era (1830–1850)

The removal era was a time when the eastern tribes were overwhelmed by pressures from whites to give up control of their lands; almost the entire southeastern Indian population was moved west in an involuntary "exchange" of their lands for western territory then considered uninhabitable by whites. The infamous "Trail of Tears" led these peoples to the region then called Indian Territory (present Oklahoma), although some did manage to remain behind. The "exchanges" were made by treaty, but they were clearly coerced (U.S. Commission on Civil Rights 1981: 19). Ironically, removal occurred shortly after the United States Supreme Court, in the so-called Cherokee Cases, had reaffirmed the principle of American Indian sovereignty. But the frontier interests, led by President Andrew Jackson, prevailed.

Mid-Century Reservations and Wars (1850–1880)

In the mid-nineteenth century the reservation system became primary in federal policy concerning Indians. Whites began to encroach upon Indian lands in all parts of the country west of the Mississippi River. Again, treaties were the instruments by which the reservations were established, involving various degrees of coercion. Unfortunately, much of the reserved land was almost simultaneously taken away through the use of "any device that was deemed effective . . . including theft, fraud, deceit, and military force" (U.S. Commission on Civil Rights 1981: 20). The so-called Indian Wars of this period were the desperate actions of groups trying to save their lands or return to homelands from reservations:

> Among the most heartrending events of Indian history are the instances when, motivated by longing for their traditional lands or by intolerable conditions on the reservations—often occasioned by failure to receive promised provisions—bands of Indians left the reservations and were pursued and sometimes slaughtered by the troops of the United States. This was the pattern behind many of the famous "battles" of the west. (Grossman 1979: 5)

In 1871, Congress included in the Appropriations Act a provision prohibiting future treaty-making with Indian tribes (25 U.S.C.A. § 71). Thereafter, reservations could only be established by executive order (although that presidential power was taken away by Congress in the early 1900s) or by act of Congress. The end of military operations and the settlement of most areas of the United States by whites resulted in a shift in the mechanisms for limiting Indian sovereignty from force and deception to the legal: executive order (short-lived), acts of Congress, and their review by the federal courts.

Assimilation and Allotment (1890–1930)

The drive to assimilate American Indians into the dominant white society intensified. One major tool of this period was the Indian boarding school movement, which removed Indian children from their familial, cultural, and social environments for the purpose of raising them according to a white way of life. The Bureau of Indian Affairs[1] assailed all elements of Indian culture on the reservations, seeking to dissolve the cohesiveness of the group. During this period, the erosion of the western tribes' traditional subsistence base forced them into economic dependency on the federal government through the Bureau of Indian Affairs. The near-fatal blow came with the General Allotment Act (the Dawes Act) of 1887 (24 Stat. 388 [1887]). Its dual purpose was to further assimilation by turning American Indians into farmers (on marginal land) and to free up "surplus" lands for white settlement. The act provided for the allotment of 160 acres to a family head and 80 acres to each single person, with title to be held in trust for 25 years. Eastern Indian Territory tribes were initially exempted, but were later subjected to similar laws.

The Indian Citizenship Act of 1924 unilaterally granted citizenship to all native-born Indians. The Meriam Report (Institute for Government Research 1928), commissioned by the federal government, was issued in 1928; it detailed the wretched conditions of Indian existence and concluded that the policy of forced assimilation had failed.

The Indian Reorganization Act of 1934, also called the Wheeler-Howard Act (48 Stat. 984 (1933–34), 25 U.S.C.A. §§ 461–479), was the culmination of the "Indian New Deal" of the Roosevelt administration and marked a major change in federal Indian policy. Although not abandoning assimilation as a goal, by this act (and others applicable only to Oklahoma tribes), Congress ended allotment, restored some of the land base, and established a revolving credit fund (never well funded) to spur economic development, among other provisions. Development was to be accomplished through each tribe's governmental organization. Tribes were encouraged to incorporate and adopt constitutions, by-laws, and law codes on the United States model, as standardized by the Bureau of Indian Affairs. This imposed governmental structure ignored traditional self-governing institutions (Grossman 1979: 25–26). Incorporation under the Reorganization Act provided unequivocal federal recognition to tribes already recognized, and allowed some previously nonrecognized tribes to become federally recognized.

THE TERMINATION PERIOD (1945–1965)

In time, Congress and the Department of the Interior determined that certain tribes were sufficiently acculturated and capable of self-government such that they could be removed from federal supervision. In 1953, the House of Representatives adopted House Concurrent Resolution 108 (1 August 1953, 67 Stat. B132), which declared the policy of termination intended to end the government-to-government relationship between the federal government and the designated tribes. The resolution's sponsors believed that this action would speed up the process of assimilation. A number of statutes enacted between 1961 and 1970 terminated two large tribes (the Menominees of Wisconsin and the Klamath of Oregon), more than seventy smaller tribes, and 37–38 rancherias in California (Cohen 1982: 811). The consequences for many of these tribes were catastrophic. Seemingly passed in the spirit of freeing American Indians from the grasp of the federal government, the termination policy was ill-conceived and allowed unscrupulous non-Indian interests a way to alienate Indian trust lands. Other acts expressing the assimilationist policy of this period increased state authority over tribes and encouraged relocation of Indians to urban areas.

The threat of wholesale termination and the nationwide focus on civil rights stimulated American Indians into political activism during the 1950s and 1960s, a time when modern Indian law and policy "came alive" (Wilkinson 1987: 7). American Indians were successful not only in stopping and partially reversing the hated termination, but also, subsequently, in building upon those gains with a series of federal statutes and favorable court decisions, although not without some setbacks.

Self-Determination (Post-1965)

The Johnson and Nixon administrations rejected the termination policy and began what has been called "self-determination," which aims at increasing tribal self-government (Grossman 1979: 28). The flagship statute of the self-determination policy was the Indian Self-Determination and Education Assistance Act of 1975 (Pub. L. 93-638, 88 Stat. 2203, 25 U.S.C.A. §§ 450–450n). That act did not, however, transfer any actual control to tribal governments, but promised "effective and meaningful participation by Indians in the administration of their affairs now under federal control" (25 U.S.C.A. § 450a[b]). Said one commentator: "While the spirit of Indian local control may appear to have been carried forward in the self-determination legislation . . . genuine control remains impossible so long as federal domination continues" (Esber 1992: 215). Federal interference has occurred when "Indian performance does not conform to the Anglo model prescribed by the government under the authority of the Secretary of the Interior" (215).

The policy of the Reagan administration has been dubbed, not so tongue-in-cheek, as "termination by accountants."

That phrase refers to the massive budget cuts in Indian programs which, according to one commentator, reflected a "blend of self-serving federal regulation, bold promises, and half-truths that left the Indian less well off than before" and "placed the sovereignty of American Indian tribes in serious jeopardy" (Morris 1992: 77).

"Self-determination" and "self-government" are distinct concepts, and Deloria and Lytle suggest that the failure to distinguish between them creates considerable misunderstanding and confusion (1984: 244). Congress has, in the last few years, moved toward encouraging more actual self-determination through increased self-government by authorizing a pilot program called the Self-Governance Demonstration Project, which is being tried out with seven tribes.

ALASKA AND HAWAII

The reach of the Indian Arts and Crafts Act apparently excludes Native Hawaiians and specifically includes Native Alaskans. The legal and political history of the Native peoples of Alaska differs greatly from those in the "lower 48"; the Alaska Natives were neither conquered militarily nor dealt with by treaty. Their aboriginal land title was extinguished only in 1971 by the provisions of the Alaska Native Claims Settlement Act (ANCSA) (Pub. L. 92-203, 43 U.S.C.A. §§ 1601–28). One writer, however, suggests that ANCSA is merely another example of the exploitative dealings of the federal government concerning aboriginal territory (Anders 1992). ANCSA set up twelve regional for-profit corporations to manage the $962.5 million dollars and forty-four million acres of land; the shareholders are all Alaskans of one-quarter blood quantum or more, born before December 18, 1971, or, where proof of blood quantum is lacking, an individual who him-or herself, or either of his or her parents, is considered a Native by his or her village or group (85, 92–93) (see chapter 4 for a discussion of "blood"). Village residents also own stock in one of the more than two hundred village corporations (92).

ANCSA's payment was compensation for the extinguishment of aboriginal land title and does not affect the eligibility of Alaskan Natives to services otherwise available to them as Indians (Cohen 1982: 769). Gary C. Anders says that the regional corporations "for all intents and purposes became the tribes of Alaska" (1992: 85).

RIGHT TO DETERMINE MEMBERSHIP

The basic power of a federally recognized Indian tribe as a sovereign entity to determine its own membership was recognized by the United States Supreme Court as early as 1897 in *Roff v. Burney* (168 U.S. 218 [1897]). It should be kept in mind that membership in a sovereign political entity is also citizenship in that entity. The modern case that reaffirms the principle that a sovereign Indian tribe should determine its own membership was brought under the Indian Civil Rights Act of 1968 (Pub. L. 90-284, 25 U.S.C.A. §§ 1301–41). The Indian Civil Rights Act made applicable to Indian tribal governments some, but not all, of the Bill of Rights that protects U.S. citizens from arbitrary and unjust actions by state and federal governments. This case, referred to in chapter 1, is *Santa Clara Pueblo v. Martinez*, decided in 1978. In that case a Pueblo woman sued her pueblo in federal court, seeking membership for her daughter, who had resided all her life in the pueblo. The daughter and her siblings were barred from membership in the Pueblo because the mother had married a Navajo man who was not a member of the Pueblo tribal group. Yet children of a Pueblo man—in other words, a male member of the tribal group—

who married out of the group were eligible for membership in the tribe. Mrs. Martinez claimed that such a membership rule based on patrilineality violated the Equal Protection provision of the Indian Civil Rights Act since it discriminated on the basis of gender and of ancestry. The court dismissed her suit, holding that the pueblo had sovereign immunity because Congress had neither expressly granted a civil action under the Indian Civil Rights Act nor could one be implied. The Indian Civil Rights Act was found applicable only to criminal cases where habeas corpus relief is expressly provided.

Many assume this ruling to be controlling in any future interpretation by a lower court of the certification provision of the Indian Arts and Crafts act; indeed, as stated by Kimberley Craven, Congressman Campbell's aide, that provision was drafted with the *Martinez* ruling in mind. Some of the principles and findings stated in the opinion are relevant. The court found that the Bill of Rights was substantially modified for application to tribal governments in furtherance of promoting the federal policy of self-determination and self-government. These modifications were made "to fit the unique political, cultural, and economic needs of tribal governments" (98 S.Ct. at 1679). Modifications include, for example, the deletion of the First Amendment prohibition against the establishment of religion inasmuch as some pueblos are theocracies. The court also found that the Indian Civil Rights Act manifested "two distinct and competing purposes," which are to protect individuals from unjust tribal authority, but also to promote tribal self-government (98 S.Ct. at 1679). Promoting self-government means protecting tribal governments from undue interference, such as review in federal court of tribal actions in civil matters. Of particular relevance to the Indian

Arts and Crafts Act, where aggrieved individuals denied certification will not be tribal members, is the principle that "tribal courts have repeatedly been recognized as appropriate forums for the exclusive adjudication of disputes *affecting important personal and property interests of both Indians and non-Indians*" (emphasis added) (98 S.Ct. at 1681).

The Indian Arts and Crafts Act of 1990 gives both state and federally recognized tribes the authority to certify artisans who are not entitled, or do not desire, to become enrolled members of the tribes. The regulations do limit this seemingly open-ended authority to certify. It is not clear how the two powers, that of the sovereign right to determine membership and that of the statutory authority to certify nonmembers, will interact. Membership in a sovereign polity is citizenship. It is clear that some of the speakers who profess concern with tribal prerogatives perceive them as linked. As noted in chapter 1, the bill's revisers wrote the certification provision to be consistent with the *Martinez* decision.

The tribes take their sovereignty very seriously. It is seen, probably correctly, as the key to the survival of each tribe as "a people" because the Indian identity is arguably not separable from the collective aspect of tribalism. This is one reason the termination policy was so hated and bitterly resisted. This is not to say that there is unanimity in individual opinions, but that most tribal Indians consider the reservation not as property, but as homeland, and the reservation system as protection against the dominant society. "Tribal sovereignty is the lifeblood of an emerging Indian separatism that permits the tribes to decide in the matters that really count: children, schools, families, crimes, finances, and land" (Wilkinson 1992: 27). Indeed, Charles H. Wilkinson (34) describes the political "Indian initiatives" of the 1950s and 1960s as being "premised on tribalism." Because sovereignty is implicit in virtually all legislation involving federally recognized tribes and their members, who are thereby also citizens, it is raised frequently in the discussion of Pub. L. 101-644 in a way that expresses the inseparability of all these conceptual distinctions. The following comments are illustrative. They were made at the congressional hearing prior to the revision that added the certification provision (U.S. House 1989a).

The chairman of the Hopi Tribal Council clearly perceives the relationship between the politics of sovereignty with the survival of tribalism and a unique Indian way of life, and the necessity of the latter for the survival of Indian arts and crafts. He relates these to the political danger of losing sovereignty should American Indians become indistinguishable from non-Indian Americans. He spoke of "the need right now to protect . . . authenticity and let's remember our people back home which is our basis of us being called an Indian tribe, our religious leaders . . . our lifeblood and who we are as people today." The chairman explained that there was a problem with misrepresentation of katcina dolls: "in order to make an authentic Kachina doll, you have to actually participate in ceremonies or know the customs of these Kachinas. Otherwise, you're going to make a Kachina that is a component of different ones put together" (76). He expressed his belief that continued sovereignty requires the continuation and strengthening of Indian identities: "Is [our sovereignty recognized] simply because we look like Indians, we speak our language, we live like Indians? . . . Once that's all gone, we are part of the mainstream of society" (76).

The general manager of the Navajo Arts and Crafts Enterprise, a tribal organization, stated that "imitation products . . . are a clear and present danger not only to our craftspeople, but to our Tribal economies, our heritage and our struggle for self-determination" (84). The executive director of the Eight Northern Pueblos Council spoke as follows:

> We strongly feel that tribes should determine who is Indian or who is recognized by the tribe. Statements were made about the Indianness of various individuals. I strongly feel and relate that to other racial and ethnic groups. I think there's a very strong distinction here. Tribes are recognized by the Federal Government as sovereign nations, and we're the only racial or ethnic group that's recognized. So I don't think it's fair to compare ethnicity and one's racial background. And so we strongly feel that tribes should determine who is a member and who is not a member, whether they're recognized by the Government or not recognized by the Government. (94)

A representative of the Native American Arts Association, based in Santa Fe and formed for the purpose of investigating fraudulent misrepresentation by artists claiming to be Indian, stated that: "We are sovereign nations, and we have a right to determine who is a member of our nation and who is a citizen of our nation. . . . We need to protect . . . [Indian art] not because of its economic impact, but for the preservation of the Indian people. You talk about culture. The majority of Native American Indian artists are involved because of culture. As a sovereign nation, we have a right to protect our own rights" (120).

The executive director of the National Congress of American Indians said that Indians have adopted the "terms of colonization" when they use the word "member" when they mean the political term "citizen"; that poor choice of term "put us on the level of the Elks or the Moose Lodge or the Boy Scouts, and that is not what we are talking about. We see this as a sovereign[ty] issue" (122–23). Her written statement accompanying the spoken testimony states that "the proposed legislation touches on several important practical and philosophical matters of intense concern to our membership, including Indian and Native national sovereignty, cultural rights and economic security, as well as the fine lines between federal protection of and interference with tribal rights and between federal protection of and imposition on the freedom of expression" (124).

She noted that the National Congress of American Indians, along with several other Indian organizations, had drafted a proposed Native American Cultural Rights Act. Its scope would be wider than arts and crafts, and it would create a civil cause of action "to make false representations for personal profit, gain or benefit, or for the profit, gain or benefit of third parties, by claiming to be a citizen of an Indian nation" (125). Such an approach "is consistent with tribal and federal law and policy . . . recognizing the inherent sovereign right of the Indian nations to determine sovereignty" (126).

No amount of sovereignty on paper alone is sovereignty exercised. Within the United States political system, how is this sovereignty put into practice? The vehicle is official "federal recognition," by the federal government, of those tribes with which it has the special government-to-government relationship. Recognition, or acknowledgment, is the subject of the next chapter. Recall that federal or state recognition is the criterion by which a "tribe" is defined in the Indian Arts and Crafts Act of 1990.

CHAPTER 3

FEDERAL AND STATE RECOGNITION

To avoid legal sanctions, the artist or craftsperson who offers his or her work for sale as Indian-produced must be an enrolled member of, or certified as an artisan by, a federally or state-recognized tribe. "Tribe" has many referents; distinguishing the most relevant may be helpful.

In anthropological terminology, "tribe" is an honorable elder, although Morton Fried says it "figures prominently on the list of putative technical terms ranked in order of degree of ambiguity as reflected in multifarious definitions" (1968: 5). Its most technical use was as a model for a form of sociopolitical organization. For example, to Julian Steward (1955), the term "tribe" is somewhat too general, but "tribal societies" are one of the "levels of socio-cultural integration" between the nuclear family and the state when perceived in terms of their different degrees of cultural complexity. To Elman Service (1962), "tribe" is a stage in an evolutionary sequence of complexity, between band and state. Fried believes the tribe is most likely a secondary phenomenon resulting from contact with more powerful societies (1968: 15). In any event, many present-day American Indian tribes do fit this latter criterion. Fried cites Elizabeth Colson's (1953) study of the Makah Tribe at Neah Bay, Washington, on the northwest coast, wherein she describes the tribe as being created from peoples of nearby, but formerly autonomous villages. "What it amounts to," says Fried, "is a tribe created by governmental action, its members showing considerable diversity in culture, language, and in physical type" (16). A number of reservations were created by removing to them the remnants of different peoples. Fried also reminds us that "so-called [contemporary] tribal groups . . . are not social organizations whose integrity recedes into a remote past; rather . . . the tribalism displayed is a reaction to more recent events and conditions" (17). Gerald Vizenor calls the results of the mix-and-match approach to historical tribal creation "simulated tribes" (1976: xxiii–xxiv).

William Sturtevant chastises Fried for adding complexity to the term "tribe," considering that it also has meaning outside the field of anthropology (1983: 10). He speaks from personal experience, having testified as an expert witness in the case of *Mashpee Tribe v. Mashpee* (477 F. Supp. 940, Mass. [1978] aff'd sub nom. *Mashpee Tribe v. New Seabury*, 592 F. 2d 557 [1st Cir. 1979]), on the issue of whether or not the Mashpee Wampanoag Tribe of Massachusetts was, in the present day, a tribe. The jury said it was not. Anthropologist Jack Campisi, also an expert witness for the tribe, wrote a book about the case, *The Mashpee Indians: Tribe on Trial* (1991). As a proponent of the contemporary Mashpee constituting a tribe in the cultural sense, and frustrated because he thinks the decision was a wrong one, he lays the fault largely (if not completely) on the manipulation of the meaning and concept of "tribe" as a legal term, albeit one derived by the court from ethnological sources. He attempts to demonstrate, in the context of this case, "the manner in which anthropological and historical data and theories were transmitted, through multiple prisms in the setting of a court, to a naive jury" (8). Those "multiple prisms" are not unique to cases involving social science, but are inherent in advocacy-based litigation.

Because "tribe" does have political connotations, Fred Gearing's 1968 definition seems useful, because it allows the flexibility required of such a concept. He defines "tribe" as a "political *array* of social boundaries" such as religious, linguistic, economic, and political, but adds, "I do not have the feeling that these various boundaries typically coincide" (1968: 111).

"Tribe" is a term in common English usage and its casual use in the past and present have created, and continue to create, misunderstandings with real consequences. Douglas R. Parks points out that the early explorers, fur traders, and other observers gave various names and spellings to the Native groups they encountered, usually attempts to record the peoples' names for themselves (1988: 170–80). This resulted in the confusion of different levels of social divisions expressed by particular terms and their haphazard use to denominate what, in these observers' Western taxonomic concepts, they believed were tribes, bands, and nations. Parks says that more conventional contemporary usages grew out of government treaty and anthropological applications, but that ambiguity is being reintroduced by American Indian activists' use of "nation," a term they feel is more consistent with their sovereignty interests, and by self-examination among anthropologists concerning their own terminology (180).

Although it is generally recognized, in retrospect, that many Indian signers of treaties did not represent "tribes," nonetheless, "in accordance with the general rule applicable to foreign treaties . . . the courts will not inquire into whether an Indian tribe was properly represented during negotiation of a ratified treaty or whether such a treaty was procured by fraud or duress" (Cohen 1982: 63).

Anthropological or legal niceties of terminology notwithstanding, past and present sociopolitical groups of Native Americans in North America are, well, tribes. There is no really satisfactory way to speak otherwise of these many polities in general, and so this book speaks of "tribes" with the hope that any particular meaning is made clear by the context.

"Tribe" is a legal term. "Tribe" has great significance in the specialized domain of Indian law. Thus "tribe" has meaning and consequences, if no precise definition. "The Indian tribe is the fundamental unit of Indian law; in its absence there is no occasion for the law to operate" (Canby 1988: 3). As noted in chapter 2, the word "tribe" appears once in the Constitution, in the Commerce Clause. It appears in treaties, as a way of identifying the signatories. Congress, with its plenary power, can both define "tribe" in federal statutes for its purposes and determine whether or not a tribe exists. Congress has created tribes by consolidating diverse groups and has split up others into multiple tribes. The United States Supreme Court, however, in *United States v. Sandoval* (231 U.S. 28 [1913]), warned that "it is not . . . that Congress may bring a community or body of people within range of this power by arbitrarily calling them an Indian tribe, but only that in respect of distinctly Indian communities the questions whether, to what extent, and for what time they shall be recognized and dealt with as dependent tribes" (231 U.S. at 46). Despite this apparent limitation, *Felix S. Cohen's Handbook of Federal Indian Law* observes that the Court has never further refined the *Sandoval* standard of "arbitrariness." It suggests that the deference of the Court to congressional and executive decisions concerning the existence of a tribe are such that the only actual requirements would be that "(a) the group have some ancestors who lived in what is now the United States before discovery by Europeans, and (b) the group be a 'people distinct from others'" (1982: 5).

The *Handbook* further observes that "tribe" has "no universal legal definition" and that there is "no single federal statute defining an Indian tribe for all purposes, although the Constitution and many federal statutes and regulations make use of the term" (3). L. R. Weatherhead suggests that Congress could make an all-purpose definition for legal purposes, but that would be unfortunate because of the great variability in social and political organization (1980: 5). Tribal existence is determined by "reference to a treaty, statute, executive order, or agreement recognizing the tribe in question [and] in other cases the definition, . . . like many other such generic terms, will depend in part on the context and the purpose for which the term is used" (Cohen 1982: 3). According to Barsh and Henderson:

> "Tribe," of course, has meaning to its members: Indian tribes are a common mental experience and natural fact for most Indians. Birth into a family, a territory, a spiritual world, and a race is a fact, but it is less significant than the mental experience that tribal people share. The essence of this mental experience is a world view—a warm, deep and lasting communal bond among all things in nature in a common vision of their proper relationship. *This consciousness cements a collective culture that has proved resilient in modern society.* (emphasis added) (1980: vii)

It is not surprising that the commingling of these many usages of "tribe" causes confusion and adds to misunderstanding and conflict. Sturtevant observes that there has been no study of the various meanings in English of terms such as "nation," "tribe," and "clan" as they are used in "ordinary conversation and writing, of legal, diplomatic, and treaty terminology, or of anthropological usage" (1983: 9). As previously noted, Sturtevant had to testify concerning whether the Mashpee were today a tribe, and he uses that case to illustrate how lawyers and judges can manipulate or misunderstand the meaning of a term which is just an ideal typological model that may, or may not, fit real societies. His solution, however, is for anthropologists to adopt a term for "tribe" that has no other English referent, possibly adopted from another language as were terms such as "totem" and "taboo" (14). This new term would probably be of limited utility in legal matters, however.

With reference to the statute under consideration in this book, any specific sociopolitical content of "tribe" is seemingly rendered irrelevant by the statutory definition that makes "tribe" a convenient cover term for tribes, bands, villages, organized groups, and, for a state-recognized entity, just "group" (25 U.S.C. § 305d [1992]; 18 U.S.C. § 1159[c][3] [1992]). However, the existence and nature of the collectivity are very much at the core of this statute, because these entities called "tribes" must be recognized by the federal or state governments, which raises the question of criteria for recognition. Furthermore, the nature of these collectivities is inextricably intertwined with concepts of American Indian identity and sovereignty, and all march forward or fall backward in tandem.

FEDERAL RECOGNITION

The current process and criteria for federal recognition are actually quite recent, dating from 1978 with the promulgation of federal regulations as set out in the *Code of Federal*

Regulations (25 C.F.R. § 83 [1993]) (see appendix C). Since 1978, six tribes have been recognized by direct congressional action and one previously terminated tribe restored (U.S. Department of the Interior 1996).

Prior to the promulgation of the present administrative scheme, federal recognition was determined from various contexts, such as tribes with reservations and tribes that had organized under the Indian Reorganization Act of 1934. In 1979, just after publication of the new regulations, a list of federally recognized tribes (except for Alaska) was published in the *Federal Register* (44 *Fed. Reg.* 7235 [1979]). The list of administratively recognized Alaskan tribes and villages was published in 1993 (58 *Fed. Reg.* 54368 [1993]). These official listings appear to simplify the determination of federally recognized tribes both before and after the 1978 regulations, in addition to any recognized by statute subsequently and in the future.

The Indian Arts and Crafts Act states that the federal type of recognition is of a tribe "eligible for the special programs and services provided by the United States to Indians because of their status as Indians." This seems to rule out any claims of de facto recognition simply because a federal statute deals with a tribe as a corporate entity. Ambiguity can always be found, however. For example, the termination acts usually had specific language proscribing further entitlement to services performed because of their status as Indian tribes. Since then, however, "several statutes have expressly included terminated tribes in special social legislation for Indians" (Cohen 1982: 813). Considering the patent unfairness of excluding the members of terminated tribes in any definition of "Indian" and the legislative history of Pub. L. 101-644, which expresses a goal of inclusion, perhaps those statutes will be interpreted in favor of the terminated tribes as de facto recognition for the purposes of the Indian Arts and Crafts Act.

The absence of a federal relationship does not imply that a group is not a "tribe in the ordinary sense" for other legal purposes (Cohen 1982: 8–9, citing *Joint Tribal Council of the Passamaquoddy Tribe v. Morton*, 528 F.2d 370 [1st Cir. (1975)]). Subsequent to that case, the Passamaquoddy did acquire federal recognition by being included in the 1979 *Federal Register* listing of recognized tribes. Also, as noted elsewhere, the tribes whose federal relationship was terminated by Congress in the 1950s and 1960s remain tribes for purposes of exercising any rights reserved by them in treaties.

Federal recognition benefits tribes in three ways: the establishment of self-government (still quite limited), eligibility (collectively and individually) for federal assistance, and the "prestige and honor in establishing the government-to-government relationship with the United States and other governmental entities, . . . an expression of their Indian pride" (Blackwell and Mehaffey 1983: 56).

The groups not recognized by the federal government are of three types: (1) those that have not yet proved that they meet the established criteria, (2) those whose petitions for acknowledgment have been denied, and (3) those that were terminated in the 1950s and 1960s and have not been restored.

The substantive (as distinct from the procedural) recognition criteria of the 1978 acknowledgment regulations issued by the Bureau of Indian Affairs, Branch of Acknowledgment and Research, require that a petitioner prove basically three things: (1) that it has existed from historic times until the present on a continuous basis and that it has been identified as Indian by various outside sources; (2) that most of its members inhabit a community or specific locale and are descended from members of an Indian tribe that historically inhabited a certain area; and (3) that it has been continuously an autonomous entity exercising political authority over its members. It also cannot be composed principally of members of other tribes or of tribes that Congress has terminated or otherwise rejected for the federal relationship status (25 C.F.R. § 83[f]&[g] [1993]. (The complete set of regulations is shown in appendix C.)

Frank W. Porter, writing in 1983, estimated that only half of the potentially eligible groups were actively pursuing the lengthy and difficult process required (ii). Preparing the documentation of the group's continuity with a known historical tribe takes years and is quite expensive; the largest expenses are for the professional services of attorneys, anthropologists, historians, and genealogists.

As of March 22, 1996, the Branch of Acknowledgment and Research has received 179 petitions. Most of these are either incomplete or mere letters of intent. The Branch has acknowledged twelve tribes and denied fourteen. Several tribes have been acknowledged by direct congressional action or dealt with by other means (U.S. Department of the Interior 1996).

Fairly or unfairly, the Branch of Acknowledgment and Research has been criticized for various alleged shortcomings. In 1991, a bill was introduced in the Senate (S. 1315, the Indian Federal Recognition Administrative Procedures Act) that would have transferred the process of acknowledgment from the Bureau of Indian Affairs to an independent commission. The commission would have been composed of three commissioners appointed by the president, with the advice and consent of the Senate. There would have been a time limit for accepting new applications for recognition: seventy-two months from the date of enactment. Senate Bill 1315 did not become law.

TERMINATION

As mentioned in chapter 2, the termination policy of the 1950s and 1960s was abandoned by the Johnson and Nixon administrations. Since that time, many tribes have been restored to their former status by federal legislation, the acknowledgment process, and, in the case of some of the rancherias, by court order.

There is no compiled list of unrestored tribes or groups, but, if the 1954 Western Oregon Termination Act (68 Stat. 724) is typical, they may be numerous. That statute terminated almost sixty "tribes" (statutorily defined as including bands, groups, and communities). The U.S. government has restored fewer than ten of those tribes, although an undetermined number were no longer in existence at the time of the legislation (Austin 1996; U.S. Department of the Interior 1995).

Those groups not yet restored are therefore not "Indian tribes," nor are their members "Indians" for the purpose of the Indian Arts and Crafts Act. In order to be "Indians" for that purpose, these individuals would have to be certified as artisans by another tribe. Yet the terminated tribes are still legally tribes for other purposes. Prior to the restoration of the Menominees, the United States Supreme Court, in *Menominee Tribe v. United States* (388 F.2d 998, 100 [ct. CL. 1967], aff'd, 391 U.S 404 [1968]), upheld the lower court's ruling that the termination act affecting this tribe did not abolish the tribe or its membership for purposes of determining the tribe's continuing treaty rights. The act served merely to terminate the federal supervision (388 F.2d at 100). *Felix S. Cohen's Handbook of Indian Law* states that further opinions have expanded this ruling such that "a terminated tribe retains all 'sovereignty authority' not inconsistent with a termination act and may continue to operate as a tribal entity for such purposes as capacity to contract, capacity to receive grants, regulation of tribal hunting and fishing rights, . . . [and it] remains an Indian tribe over which Congress has the authority to legislate . . . [including] passing restoration legislation reversing the effects of the original termination acts" (Cohen 1982: 19) (citations omitted).

STATE RECOGNITION

State recognition is a process entirely independent of federal recognition. Ten states, all in the East, have recognized "tribes" to date. Criteria range from strict to none, mostly the latter. The other states do not formally recognize American Indian tribes independently from federal recognition. Those states where federally recognized tribes are located do, of course, formally or informally acknowledge them, but that has no relevance to this study and will not be further discussed. In most of the states discussed below, there are additional groups that have petitioned for federal recognition and, presumably, are also candidates for state recognition.

In Florida, the Governor's Council on Indian Affairs (1988) adopted a policy which recommends that state officials refrain from recognizing any group not first acknowledged by the federal government. A secondary set of recommendations sets out criteria for state recognition in the event that the first recommendation is ignored. It suggests that such state action should (1) create a government-to-government relationship between state and tribe, (2) set forth an explicit rendering of the state's interpretation of "recognition," (3) be confined only to groups descended from Seminole, Miccosukee, Creek, or a tribe located in

Florida prior to May 30, 1830, and (4) meet federal criteria for recognition. The Florida legislature has not since acted on these matters.[1]

The State of Maryland has no federal or state-recognized tribes. The legislature has authorized a commission on Indian affairs (Article 83B, § 5-406[b], Annotated Code of Maryland) to promulgate regulations for recognition, and has issued detailed procedural requirements and criteria for attaining state recognition (COMAR 05.08.06). Two groups, both claiming Piscataway antecedents, have pending applications for recognition by Maryland.[2]

The New Mexico State Constitution authorizes the state to recognize tribes other than those with federal recognition, but this has not been pursued by the New Mexico legislature.

STATES WITH STATE-RECOGNIZED TRIBES[3]

Alabama

Alabama has seven state-recognized tribes, all recognized by 1984 acts, Nos. 84–257, effective May 8, 1984 (Code of AL 41-9-708). Criteria for the recognition of additional tribes are set forth in Administrative Rule 475-x-3-03.[4]

Only one of the seven tribes is federally recognized, the Poarch Band of Creek Indians, in Atmore, Alabama. The other six are:

1. Cherokees of Northeast Alabama (Collinsville, Ala.)
2. Cherokees of Southeast Alabama (Evergreen, Ala.)
3. Echota Cherokee Tribe of Alabama (Birmingham, Ala.)
4. Machis Lower Creek Indian Tribe (New Brockton, Ala.)
5. MOWA Band of Choctaw Indians (Mt. Vernon, Ala.) (MOWA is derived from Mobile-Washington)
6. Star Clan of Muscogee Creek Indians (Goshen, Ala.)

Of these groups, three have applied for federal acknowledgment. The Machis Lower Creek Tribe's petition was denied in 1988. The Department of the Interior published proposed negative findings for the MOWA Band, but the comment period is, at this writing, still open. In 1988, the Cherokees of Southeast Alabama filed a letter of intent to petition (U.S. Department of the Interior 1996).

Connecticut

Connecticut has five state-recognized tribes, two of which are also federally acknowledged—the Mashantucket Pequot (Ledyard, Conn.) and the Mohegan Tribe (Uncasville, Conn.). All state recognition was statutory, by enactments in October 1973. Although the state has no criteria for recognition, the state's Indian Affairs coordinator states that there is documentation of a state-tribal relationship for each tribe since colonial times.[5] The three tribes with state recognition only are:

1. Golden Hill Paugussett (Trumbull, Conn.)
2. Schaghticoke (Monroe, Conn.)
3. Paucatuck Eastern Pequot (North Stonington, Conn.)

All three petitioned for federal recognition. The Interior Department published proposed negative findings on the Golden Hill Paugussett in June 1996. The Schaghticoke and Paucatuck Eastern Pequot tribes have filed incomplete federal petitions. The Acknowledgment Branch acts only upon completely documented petitions (U.S. Department of the Interior 1996).

Delaware

Delaware has no federally recognized tribes and only one state-recognized tribe—the Nanticoke Tribe.[6] It is questionable, however, whether the Nanticoke constitute a tribe for the purposes of the Indian Arts and Crafts Act because the enabling state legislation has limited applicability. This legislation reads as follows:

> (a) The class of people known as the descendants of the Nanticoke Indians, formerly of Sussex County but at present located in the several counties of this State, who desire to migrate, may appear before any justice of the peace or notary public of this State and, on the evidence and proof that he belongs to or is a descendant of the Nanticoke Indians, may procure from such justice or notary a certificate reciting such facts.
>
> (b) The descendants of the Nanticoke Indians named in subsection (a) of this section shall be recognized as such within this State. (Del. Code Ann. tit. 29, § 105 [1993]).

These provisions appear to affect only individuals and presumably do not recognize tribes as corporate groups; thus it is questionable whether the legislation would be read as state recognition under the Indian Arts and Crafts Act. The Nanticokes have sent to the Branch of Acknowledgment and Research a letter of intent to petition (U.S. Department of the Interior 1996).

Georgia

Georgia has no federally recognized tribes. It recognizes three state tribes by statute (GA. CODE ANN. § 44-12-300(a) [1993]) and provides in section b of that statute for recognition of tribes, bands, groups, or communities "as the General Assembly deems appropriate." There are no official criteria. The state-recognized tribes are:[7]

1. Georgia Tribe of Eastern Cherokee (Dahlonega, Ga.)
2. Lower Muscogee Creek Tribe (Whigham, Ga.)
3. Cherokee of Georgia Tribal Council (Saint George, Ga.)

The petition of the Lower Muscogee Creek Tribe for federal acknowledgment was denied. The Georgia Tribe of Eastern Cherokee was notified of "obvious deficiencies" in its petition (U.S. Department of the Interior 1996).

Louisiana

Louisiana has five tribes recognized by state legislative action, in addition to four federally recognized tribes: the (1) Chitimacha (Charenton, La.), (2) Coushatta (Elton, La.), (3) Jena Band of Choctaws (Jena, La.), and (4) the Tunica-Biloxi (Mansura, La.).[8] There are no official criteria or procedures for state recognition. The state-recognized tribes recognized by legislative resolutions are:

1. Apache Choctaw (Zwolle, La.)
2. Clifton Choctaw (Gardner, La.)
3. Louisiana Band of Choctaw (Baker, La.)
4. United Houma Nation, Inc. (Golden Meadow, La.)
5. Caddo Adais (Robeline, La.)

The Branch of Acknowledgment and Research published proposed negative findings on the Houmas' petition, with the comment period still open. In September 1995, a group calling themselves the "Biloxi, Chitimacha Confederation of Muskogees, Inc." withdrew from the Houmas and plans to respond separately to those proposed negative findings. The Apache Choctaw, Caddo Adais, and Clifton Choctaw have all submitted either incomplete petitions or letters of intent to petition for federal recognition (U.S. Department of the Interior 1996).

Massachusetts

In addition to one federally recognized tribe, the Gay Head Wampanoag, there are three state-recognized tribes in Massachusetts:[9]

1. Nipmuc Tribal Council of Massachusetts (Grafton, Mass.)
2. Mashpee Wampanoag Tribe (Mashpee, Mass.)
3. Heron Pond Wampanoag Tribe (Heron Pond, Mass.)

Four more of the numerous Wampanoag groups are reorganizing. That will allow them to be "recognized" by the state's Indian Affairs Council without further process or procedure, inasmuch as there is a history of governmental dealings with the separate groups (or bands or tribes) from colonial days.[10] Remedial state legislation may be necessary to make these groups state-recognized for the purposes of the Indian Arts and Crafts Act. The Mashpee Wampanoags' land unit claim, as mentioned earlier, was unsuccessful, but they have filed a petition for federal acknowledgment, which is considered complete and awaiting consideration. The Nipmuc have filed two federal petitions, by groups calling themselves the Hassanamisco Band and the Chaubunagungamaub Band, on which proposed findings are pending (U.S. Department of the Interior 1996).

North Carolina

North Carolina contains one federally recognized tribe, the Eastern Band of Cherokee Indians, Cherokee, North Carolina. The Lumbee, of Pembroke, North Carolina, have an anomalous type of federal *non*recognition, which is described in chapter 5.

Under statutory authority legislated in 1976 (N.C. GEN. STAT. §143B–406), the North Carolina Commission on Indian Affairs established procedures and criteria for state recognition (N.C. Admin Code TO 1:15.0200). The commission provided for two types of recognition: as an "Indian tribe" or as an "Indian organization or group" (§ .0208). The first is "a population of Indian people all related to one another by blood, tracing their heritage to Indians [*sic*] tribes indigenous to North Carolina within the last 200 years." The latter is "a population of Indian people made up of members of state or federally recognized tribes . . . [of which] ninety percent of the organization or group must be Indian" (§ .0208). A group petitioning for tribal status must meet five of the eight listed criteria, which are:

1. Traditional North Carolina Indian names
2. Kinship relationships with other recognized tribes
3. Official records such as birth, church, school, or other documents recognizing the people as Indian
4. Letters or statements from state or federal authorities recognizing the people as Indian
5. Anthropological or historical accounts tied to the tribe's ancestry
6. Letters or statements from presently recognized tribes or groups or their representatives attesting to the Indian heritage of the tribe
7. Any other documented traditions, customs, legends, etc., that signify the tribe's Indian heritage
8. Participation in, or grants from, sources or programs designated as for Indians only

Despite these listed criteria, Section .0205 states that the commission "may . . . in its discretion" recognize a tribe. Unless this section has already been interpreted otherwise, it suggests the commission may have discretionary authority to ignore the criteria. The Lumbee Tribe's state recognition precedes the establishment of those criteria; I have not been able to obtain information concerning whether the other tribes did meet them.

The North Carolina state-recognized tribes are:[11]

1. Lumbee (Pembroke, N.C.)
2. Haliwa Saponi (Hollister, N.C.)
3. Coharie (Clinton, N.C.)

4. Waccamaw Siouan (Bolton, N.C.)
5. Meherrin (Winton, N.C.)

The Lumbee Tribe's attempts to obtain federal recognition are described in chapter 5. The Haliwa Saponi Tribe has been notified of "obvious deficiencies" in its federal petition, and the Coharie, Waccamaw Siouan, and two separate Meherrin tribes have all submitted undocumented letter petitions (U.S. Department of the Interior 1996).

Patricia Barker Lerch mentions the "Indians of Person County" as a tribe or group recognized by the state in 1913 (1992: 46, 48).

New York

New York has seven federally recognized tribes and an additional two state-recognized tribes, the latter by authority of Indian Law articles 9 and 10, respectively[12]. The two state-recognized tribes are:

1. Shinnecock Tribe (Southampton, N.Y.)
2. Poospatuck (Ynkechauge) Indian Nation (Mystic, N.Y.)

The Shinnecock Tribe has submitted a letter of intent to petition to the Acknowledgment and Research Branch for federal recognition (U.S. Department of the Interior 1996).

Tennessee

The Etowah Cherokee Nation, headquartered in Cleveland, claims to be state-recognized under authority of a proclamation by the governor of Tennessee dated May 25, 1978. That document proclaims that "I, Ray Blanton, as Governor of the State of Tennessee, do hereby officially recognize the Etowah Cherokee Nation in the State of Tennessee as a Nation of People" (Indian Arts and Crafts Board, Files 1991). In its provisions concerning state-recognition, the Indian

Arts and Crafts Act specifically refers to recognition by "a State *legislature* or by a State commission or similar organization *legislatively* vested with State tribal recognition authority" (emphasis added) (25 U.S.C. § 305d[4] [1992]). I suspect the governor's proclamation was merely one of those meaningless "feel-good" actions that politicians use to make constituents happy. The Tennessee legislature did create a Commission of Indian Affairs to provide for recognition of individuals and groups, but not tribes. Concerning the Etowah, the commission takes the position that the group is only a "legally chartered non-profit Indian-related organization," and that there are no statutes "authorizing the governor to recognize certain Native Americans as a nation of people."[13] After a public hearing in 1993, the commission voted to discontinue providing recognition to individuals stating that they were Indian.[14]

Thus, except for the governor's proclamation, Tennessee has no state-recognized tribes, nor does it have any federally recognized tribes. The Etowah have sent a letter of intent to petition to the Branch of Acknowledgment seeking federal recognition and must prepare the documentation in order to be considered (U.S. Department of the Interior 1996).

Virginia

There are no federally recognized tribes in Virginia, but the state has recognized eight. The state-recognized tribes are, according to Helen C. Rountree (1992: 10–11):

1. Pamunkey Indian Tribe (King William, Va.)
2. Mattaponi Indian Tribe (West Point, Va.)
3. Upper Mattaponi Indian Tribal Association (St. Stephen's Church, Va.)
4. Chickahominy Indian Tribe (Providence Forge, Va.)

5. Chickahominy Tribe, Eastern Division (Providence Forge, Va.)
6. United Rappahannock Tribe (Indian Neck, Va.)
7. Nansemond Indian Tribal Association (Chesapeake, Va.)
8. Monacan Indian Tribal Association (Monroe, Va.)

The Pamunkey and Mattaponi have reservations reserved through colonial-era treaties that were ratified by the Commonwealth in 1658 (Kickingbird and Ducheneaux 1973: 209). Despite their "virtually impeccable title," these groups have never received benefits from the federal government (209). The Pamunkey Tribe's attorney told Congress, in 1991, that the tribe's state reservation originated in the tribe's treaty with the Crown in the 1600s and has been occupied by Pamunkey Indians since that time, under strict residency requirements, and that they have continuously had a tribal council. Furthermore, the treaty obligated them to provide "to the Crown a deer every year, and they've done that. Since Virginia became a Commonwealth, they gave a deer to the Governor of the Commonwealth . . . every single year" (U.S. Senate 1991a: 61).

The other state-recognized tribes do not have reservations. They were recognized at various times by resolutions of the Virginia General Assembly, which appointed a subcommittee in the early 1980s to study the matter (Rountree 1992: 26).

State recognition in Virginia means only that the group is formally organized (a corporation) with a tribal roll; it does not imply comment on its status in colonial times (Rountree 1992: 26). "The only thing it does is to bolster the credibility of Indian groups seeking federal moneys for community development and the like" (26).

The Mattaponi, Monacan, United Rappahannock, and Upper Mattaponi Tribes have filed letters of intent to petition for federal recognition (U.S. Department of the Interior 1996). Rountree notes, however, that continuous documentation is a problem in Virginia inasmuch as many county records were burned during the Civil War and at other times (1992: 11).

The Southeastern Indians

The southeastern aboriginal peoples were among the earliest to confront the leading edge of European incursion; they suffered perhaps the greatest amount of depopulation and social disruption from early white settlement, and they bore the brunt of the federal removal policy of the 1830s. In recent decades an awareness has developed that perhaps more of these groups did survive than earlier was believed, although the great degree of assimilation and triracial mixing has created a very complex situation indeed. This complexity has contributed to the phenomenon of the state-recognized tribe, as distinct from the better known federal recognition status.

To complicate the situation, some of the groups that claim to be "Indian" probably fit what, in less politically correct times, were called "triracial isolates," "marginal peoples," and other such terms (Griessman 1972: 693). The commonality of these groups is "the idea of apartness, whether genetic or social" (693). Dane and Griessman explore the conditions that resulted in collective identities for these groups of unknown origin, but for which "whatever questions may exist about their origins and racial composition, there can be no doubt about their own claim to be Indians." Their known histories, especially since the Civil War, show "an enormous amount of energy . . . expanded in simply maintaining a recognized Indian status in the face of the ever-present possibility of being submerged into a general non-white community" (695). This process, which for some has been successful, is what Karen I. Blu means by the title of her book *The Lumbee Problem: The Making of an American Indian People* (1980). Calvin Beale's "mixed racial isolates" are "real or alleged White-Indian-Negro mixtures . . . who are not tribally affiliated or traceable with historical continuity to a particular tribe" (1972: 705). These groups are distributed widely throughout the eastern and southern regions of the United States; the existence of some can be documented since pre-Revolutionary times. The key factors that bear upon the social acceptance and legal recognition of these groups as Indian include their separateness as a genetic and ethnic group and their consistent efforts over time to avoid being considered black, the latter strategy focusing on development of an identity as Indian (Beale 1972).

Susan Greenbaum takes issue with the interpretation that these groups originated as "residual by-products of the south's biracial caste system—involuntary aggregates of outcastes" rather than reflecting the "voluntary cohesion and shared traditions associated with Indian tribes" (1991: 13). The racial nature of these studies, she argues, has influenced, or at least supported, the improper injection of race into the question of whether a particular group is an Indian tribe.

George Roth (1992) summarizes the current status of the groups and tribes in the Southeast, noting their great variety in size and character and in the degree of retention, loss, or merely lack of traditional Indian culture traits. He distinguishes between those groups with "clear-cut and accepted tribal origins and identities and ones whose Indianness or specific tribal origins presently or in the past have been the subject of debate and disagreement with non-Indians and sometimes other tribes" (183). Tribes in the first category include those such as the Poarch Creek (Alabama) and the Tunica-Biloxi (Louisiana), both of which were successful in obtaining federal recognition. Those with questionable origins include the Lumbee (North Carolina) and many others (183). With continued research, perhaps some of the groups in the latter category will move to the first. An example from the Northeast is the Abenaki. David Ghere shows that the "disappearance" of the this tribe from western Maine was the result of assumptions made by "colonial observers and early historians [who] assumed a tribal organization for the Abenaki with each tribe occupying a river drainage area," a model that has since been accepted by modern historians (1993: 193). Ghere argues, however, that the Abenaki social structure prior to white incursion was one of dispersed family bands that periodically congregated in large gatherings for social and ritual purposes. In response to pressures from expanding white settlement, they stopped gathering in large camps and spent the entire year in small camps or villages, thus becoming invisible to the whites. The "English observers assumed that the absence of tribal villages meant the abandonment of the area and that the family bands were merely hunters" from other areas (204).

On the other hand, human nature being what it is, states without any criteria for recognition lay themselves open to the charlatan groups that can obtain recognition solely through political manipulation. In a state without recognition criteria, and where no obligations are incurred by the state, it is a relatively simple political maneuver for a state legislator to satisfy a group of constituents by sponsoring a resolution declaring them an Indian tribe—resulting in a win-win situation.

There are three federally recognized Cherokee tribes in the United States: the Eastern Band of Cherokee Indians, headquartered in Cherokee, North Carolina; the Cherokee Nation of Oklahoma, in Talequah, Oklahoma; and the United Keetoowah Band of Cherokee Indians, also in Oklahoma. The former principal chief of the Cherokee Nation of Oklahoma wrote letters in 1992 to several state governors expressing the "growing concern . . . developing on behalf of responsible Cherokee officials and tribal members regarding the claims of other purported 'Cherokee' groups" seeking federal or state recognition. She requested that the states make federal recognition a prerequisite to state recognition inasmuch as dealing with Indian tribes has always been exclusively restricted to the federal government, the process of obtaining federal recognition is arduous, and the proliferation of "Indian tribes is confusing to the public." She provided a list of entities using the Cherokee name (Mankiller 1992). A number of these groups have already been recognized by their respective states.

Jonathan Taylor, principal chief of the Eastern Band of Cherokee (North Carolina), spoke to the Senate's Select Committee on Indian Affairs:

> There are many people in our country—including an inordinate percentage of whom live in the Southeast—that have varying degrees of Indian blood in their veins. . . . There are, without question, hundreds of thousands of people in the Southeast and in Oklahoma who have some degree of Cherokee ancestry and who are proud of this ancestry. . . . If you were to take every community in the Southeast with a sizable population of Cherokee descendants—even if you

> narrowed it down to only those communities with Indian Clubs or organizations in them—and suggest that each was somehow a tribe, the country would have dozens and perhaps hundreds of Cherokee Tribes. (U.S. Senate 1991a: 105)

Roth discusses the claims in recent years of groups claiming Indian status—groups that have formed organizations for that purpose but that have no past history to substantiate their claims. He suggests these are made up mostly of lower-middle-class and lower-class whites attracted by the current benefits of being proclaimed Indian (1992: 200–201). Two of the groups he mentions have, in fact, obtained state recognition—the Machis Creek (Alabama) and the Lower Muscogee Creek (Georgia). Two groups calling themselves the Lower Muskogee Creek Nation East of the Mississippi and the Principal Creek Nation were refused federal acknowledgment because, although their members had some Creek ancestry, there was no proof of tribal history or tribal social or political organization (200–201). The Machis Creek, recognized by the State of Alabama, were determined by the federal Acknowledgment Office to have neither substantial Indian ancestry (Creek or otherwise) nor any existence as a collectivity of any sort prior to the 1980s (201). The Machis are one of several groups denied acknowledgment in accordance with the administrative criteria. The summary of their case, as published by the Branch of Acknowledgment and Research (52 Fed. Reg. 34319–20 [1987]), serves as an illustration:

> The Machis Lower Alabama Creek Indian Tribe contends that it is descended from those Creek Indians who took land allotments rather than move to Indian Territory in the 1830s and that their ancestors purportedly then fled to a cave in

Covington County, Alabama, to hide from hostile whites and soldiers. No documentation has been found to substantiate the existence of a predecessor tribe or Indian community to the group. The Machis Lower Alabama Creek Indian Tribe has only been identified as Indian and as Creek since its incorporation as a non-profit corporation in 1982. The tribe which inhabited the Lower Creek town of Tamali, which the group claims was the aboriginal home of the "Machis Indians", emigrated to northwestern Florida around the year 1800 and was absorbed in the Seminole tribe. No historical reference could be found to document the existence of a Lower Creek Indian named Machis, who[m] the group claims descent from and from whom the group derives its name. No evidence could be found to verify linkage between the early 19th-century Lower Creek individuals in Alabama whom the petitioner claims were its ancestors and the family lines of the group's membership.

The group holds that its ancestors managed to escape forced removal from Alabama by hiding in a cave in Covington County. Federal census records indicate that most of the group's ancestors did not take up residence in Alabama until long after the period of Creek removal and that none of the primary families were living in Covington County prior to the 1880s. While federal census and county records show there has been some residential clustering and interaction among the principal families in the group from 1850 to the present at various and somewhat scattered locations in southeastern Alabama, these family enclaves have never been regarded by others as being American Indian communities. There is no evidence that tribal political influence or authority has been exercised or maintained over its members or that tribal decision-making processes have been carried out by group leaders either prior to or after the formal incorporation of the group in 1982. . . . Although the majority of the membership does share common ancestry,

> no documentation was submitted nor was any documentation located to establish that the common ancestors of the group were identified as Indian or were members of any historical tribe or tribes.

Porter, like Greenbaum, argues that, until recently, research on the eastern communities has been "biased because of their interpretation . . . as tri-racial isolates, not necessarily as descendants of Indians" (1983: 37). This interpretation incorporated the public opinion and prejudices of the area rather than being based on information contained within the Indian community itself. This led, he argues, to distortions of the "essential processes involved in the persistence of the Indian communities to the present" (37). Because the studies focused on surviving aboriginal culture traits or on the ramifications of being triracial isolates, they did not address the most important question, "whether and to what extent these groups are Indian" (37–38). The remedy is to address the "process of acculturation, the reconstruction of tribal histories, the economic and social integration of Indians into White society, and the problems related to maintaining tribal identity and achieving federal recognition" (38). Porter characterizes nonrecognition as a "negative aspect of federal Indian policy" that resulted from the fact that these groups became "forgotten people," at least until the Passamaquoddy of Maine successfully litigated their land claims and stimulated a revival of interest in other eastern groups (43).

The degree of assimilation is legally irrelevant once a tribe has been granted federal recognition, although it may pose political danger, as was demonstrated by the termination policy. There is, however, an unresolved legal problem concerning assimilation and the continued existence of a group seeking recognition as a tribe. The legal question turns on whether a tribe that has dissolved through involuntary assimilation has abandoned its claim to federal recognition (Weatherhead 1980: 43–46).

Nationwide, the census of self-reported Indian population grew 38 percent between 1980 and 1990. The rate of growth was "predictable . . . in the nineteen 'Indian states' . . . [but] soared in the non-Indian states" (Fost 1991: 34). The largest increase was in Alabama, which experienced a 117 percent increase, from 7,600 to 16,500 between 1980 and 1990 (34). This is explained by Dan Fost as the resurgence of Indian pride amongst part-Indians, who became more willing to identify themselves (34). In her book *American Indian Ethnic Renewal*, Joane Nagel examines the dramatic increase in Indian self-identification, which cannot be explained through normal demographic factors. She draws the conclusion that many individuals newly identify themselves as Indians as a result of the Indian ethnic resurgence stimulated by the Red Power activism of the 1960s and 1970s (1996).

The next chapter will describe and discuss the question of American Indian identity, which is at the heart of the problem under analysis.

CHAPTER 4

THE IDENTITY QUESTION

Who, and what, is an American Indian? These are distinct concepts—"Who" is a matter of identification, "what," a matter of identity. Before the arrival of the Europeans in the Western Hemisphere, there were no "Indians" by any name, that is, as a general designation for all of the inhabitants. When the Europeans arrived on the shores of what they initially believed was India and called the people they encountered Indians, the "who" was easy—anyone who was an aboriginal inhabitant. But the discovery of the "New World" meant that the "what" was a little trickier, a matter of such consequence as to command learned debate at the highest levels of Christendom. As soon, however, as the first European-American Indian offspring arrived, presumably very quickly, the question of identity began to accumulate complexities, an ongoing process throughout the intervening centuries and one that will continue for future generations to ponder. Today, the who and what have become tangled, with often nonsensical consequences: One is an "Indian" only if one can prove one is.

Despite the large amount of literature on ethnicity and ethnic groups, surely no one would claim that American Indians are not "ethnic." They are quick to point out, however, that because of their legal status they are not simply another domestic minority. The only question is, To what extent are they a single ethnic group and to what extent are they multiple ethnic groups reflecting the great diversity of tribal groups? Nagel discusses this question in terms of tribal and "supratribal" Indian identity (1996). The complex answers to this question are beyond the scope of this book, but the basic question of Indian identity *is* relevant here, especially to the determination as to who and what an Indian is, particularly with respect to individuals without tribal connections who may acquire their ethnic content from exposure to pan-Indian traits.

The Indian Arts and Crafts Act of 1990 simplifies both the identity and identification questions. An Indian is any individual with the requisite relationship to a designated political entity; his or her identification is merely a matter of simple documentation by that entity. This simplified definition, however, is why the statute is problematical.

The nineteenth century was, as might be expected, a time of foment in the formulation of Indian identity—legally, politically, and in the public's perception. Indian identity was a key component in the legislating of the Dawes Act of 1887 and its consequences. Full-blood Indian populations declined dramatically during the nineteenth century, and mixed-blood populations increased (Unrau 1989: 2). The Dawes Act created a need to consider who or what an Indian is, especially since many whites and blacks claimed to be Indian in order to obtain allotments of land.

In the early nineteenth century, an "Indian" was an individual with some Indian blood or one accepted as an Indian by his or her tribe. The use of terms concerning "blood," such as "full-blood," "mixed-blood," "blood quantum," and related quantitative terms such as "half-breed," are in common and legal usage because they are well understood even if without scientific basis. Indeed, this kind of categorization is apparently so ingrained among contemporary American Indians that it is not uncommon for a full-blood to refer to himself or herself as "four-fourths Indian." Demographer Matthew C. Snipp tells us that "historically, 'blood quantum' has a been central concept in administrative definitions," a leftover from the nineteenth-century belief that "blood was the carrier of genetic material and cultural traits" (1989: 32). In spite of its being easily understood as conveying information about ancestry, if not other attributes, Snipp observes that "the use of blood quantum to define the modern Indian population poses enormous conceptual and practical problems" (44).

By the late 1800s the Indian tribes were recognized as the appropriate authorities for determining their own membership. Congressman Charles Curtis (later vice-president in the administration of President Hoover) was himself a mixed-blood (Kansa-Kaw-white) and sensitive to the concerns of mixed-bloods. His goal was to facilitate assimilation by encouraging rather than penalizing mixed marriages. The goal of assimilation, however, was not and is not considered desirable by many American Indians (Unrau 1989: 1). William E. Unrau tells us that "Curtis also recognized that Congress could make or unmake an Indian, regardless of genealogy, ethnological data, treaty commitments, or tribal preferences. So could an employee of the Indian office, acting under his interpretation of federal law or the directive of an administrative superior" (3). Curtis introduced legislation in 1896 to give the children of white men and American Indian women equal rights to tribal property as tribal members (1). It failed to pass, thus leaving the matter of determining the identity of most mixed-bloods to "legislative relief at the individual and tribal levels, expensive legal action, or intense maneuvering and lobbying within the tribal political structures" (6).

In the present day, James L. Simmons suggests six types of definitions of Indian people (1977: 78):

1. Legal definitions
2. Self-declaration, such as the self-reporting method of the U.S. Census
3. Community recognition
4. Recognition as an Indian by non-Indians
5. Biological definitions, such as that reflected in the Certificates of Degree of Indian Blood and CDIB cards issued by the Bureau of Indian Affairs, Department of the Interior.
6. Cultural definitions that depend on "however culture may be defined by Indians or others."

There is no single definition of "Indian" in federal law just as there is none for "tribe." The Constitution and many statutes do not contain definitions. Many other statutes define Indians as members of federally recognized tribes, which themselves show great variation in membership criteria, and many also contain definitions that require a specific blood quantum. As *Felix S. Cohen's Handbook of Federal Indian Law* summarizes this situation:

> Some people . . . can be an Indian for one purpose but not for another. A Caucasian or person of little Indian ancestry might become a tribal member by adoption for some purposes, such as voting and participation in tribal government, but not be an Indian for purposes of federal criminal jurisdiction. An Indian whose tribe has been terminated will not be considered an Indian for most federal purposes. Nevertheless, such a person remains an Indian ethnologically and continues to be a tribal member for internal tribal purposes.

> Furthermore, a member of a terminated tribe will be considered an Indian for the purposes of those federal programs which are available to all Indians, including members of terminated tribes. Thus, although many persons are Indians for all purposes, status as an Indian depends upon the circumstances involved. (Citations omitted) (1982: 26–27)

A different perspective on this inexactitude is offered by Frances Svensson (1979: 71). The identity question is, she says, always contextual, depending on who is asking and why. The need to determine who would be eligible for federal governmental services required formulation of legal concepts of Indian identity, a process in which both the tribes and the federal government had "a direct stake" (72). As evidenced by the Indian Arts and Crafts Act, nontribal individuals have a stake as well, one at odds with the basic underlying assumptions Svensson attributes to the approaches of both tribes and government. These basic assumptions are that "individual and communal status can and should be distinguished, and that Indian identity is at some point and in some circumstances alienable" (72). Both non-Indian and Indian approaches tend to "reserve Indian status for those who remain part of an Indian community, eliminating those who, whatever their 'racial' background, have left it." This requires the establishment of "boundary criteria . . . to mark the place at which diminished Indian blood, culture, political affinity, etc., indicate the transition from an Indian to an American identity. This is the point at which Indian identity is alienated" (73). Expression of this perspective is found in tribal membership criteria, which often combine descent and residence requirements, and by the federal government in requirements that there be some blood quantum and that the individual be considered an Indian by his community (73).

In the 1990 census, 1,878,285 Americans identified themselves as American Indians, 57,152 as Eskimos, and 23,797 as Aleuts (U.S. Bureau of the Census 1990: 3). Since 1960, census procedures required that Americans classify themselves by race (Thornton 1987: 216). The initiation of self-reporting resulted in an increase in the Indian population of almost 50 percent between 1950 and 1960, with further increases in each subsequent census, raising the issue as to "how much of the increase was valid and true rather than due simply to self-reporting" (220; U.S. Bureau of the Census 1990: 3). Among the explanations offered for the dramatic difference are: (1) an earlier failure to identify non-reservation Indians, (2) the inclusion of individuals not Indians for other purposes, (3) undercounting of Indians on reservations, and (4) change in self-identification (Thornton 1987: 220–23). Russell Thornton suggests that an "enumeration procedure reflecting individual self-definition . . . seems the most reasonable method yet devised, though it is fraught with problems" (222). He concludes that:

> In important ways, the twentieth-century American Indian population recovery has been related to changing definitions of American Indians, and . . . changes in how American Indians were enumerated in U.S. censuses. Only in part, it seems, was the recovery a result of the fundamental demographic processes of births, deaths, and migrations. . . . Even the direct implications of biological mixing . . . may not account for all of the recovery. *Rather, biological mixing resulted in a need to change definitions of American Indians,* which in turn somewhat expanded population numbers. This seems especially true of the American Indian population since 1960, when self-definition has been used in census enumerations. (Emphasis added) (223–24)

Snipp suggests that self-identification, unlike blood quantum definitions, is free of assumptions about what race is, thus allowing each person to decide for himself or herself and to determine what information to utilize for self-classification (1989: 36). With this method, however, no one can tell what an individual means by Indian when he or she selects that category of self-identification (37). It is ironic that the value expressed by so many—that American Indians should define themselves—has two completely different and contradictory aspects: self-identification by individuals and collective self-identification by groups calling themselves tribes, which then claim to be the sole authorities in the determination of which individuals qualify as Indians.

Most modern writers on ethnicity, however, agree that there are objective as well as subjective aspects to ethnicity; there are "wannabee" tribes as well as "wannabee" individuals. In discussing the census and the procedure whereby Americans select their own classifications, Thornton states that:

> what seems important . . . is that American Indians be allowed to do their own defining, either as individuals or as tribes. This may occur on the individual level through self-identification; it may occur on the tribal level through formal membership. One may object that self-identification allows considerable variation among individuals defined as American Indian, but American Indians have always had tremendous variation among themselves, and the variations in many ways have been increased, not reduced, by the events of history, demographic and other. Allowing self-identification and the differences it encompasses is simply to allow American Indians to be American Indians, something done all too infrequently in the short history of the United States. (1987: 224)

In any event, presumably no objective view today recognizes that a smidgen of Indian ancestry alone makes an Indian. If it did, the Indian population in the United States would swell to the more than seven million Americans (more than one of every thirty-five) who, according to one demographer, claim some Indian ancestry (Fost 1991: 28). That perception of what an Indian is would make Indian identity and status meaningless.

Rayna Green, in her essay "The Tribe Called Wannabee" (1988: 42, 44), discusses the fascination of white Americans (and Europeans) with "playing Indian," from wearing the "Santa Fe Chic" clothing style to the victory dance and victory yell of the Washington Redskins's mascot. She includes those individuals who, for commercial reasons, engage in "lifelong impersonation." She speaks of writers, actors, and "gurus"; her comments apply equally to artists and craftspeople. Because the "persona of Indian has always been a compelling one, . . . some have rarely wanted to or been able to separate that persona from their real biographical self" (44). Among current celebrity "Indians," she notes writers William Least Heat Moon and Jamake Highwater (45).

More difficult to reconcile and define is the case of the self-proclaimed mixed-bloods. Green suggests that the significance of "mestizoization" led to the development of a "cult" for the process and its results. One of those results is "a curious form of racial politics in the claiming of 'Indian Blood,' a fictional mixed-blood world" (46).

For many whites who claim Indian descent, usually from a "Cherokee princess," this is a casual and social matter without connection to their livelihood, although some would like to get government benefits (460). However, for "Blacks and Hispanics, both in and outside of the United States, the claim is deeply rooted in racial politics" (46).

(This aspect was noted in the discussion of state-recognized tribes in chapter 3.) Green continues:

> The claiming of Indian blood is so common among Blacks in America that Langston Hughes, the poet, even devoted verse to it in his series of poems featuring the folk-philosopher Simple, where Simple makes fun of those blacks who need to claim Indian blood in order to relieve themselves of the burden of being solely Black, or, as in the case of most Black Americans, a mixture of Black, white and other races. Blacks also most often claim to have Cherokee blood, but as well Blackfeet blood . . . . The assertion, unsubstantiated by any known familial or settlement pattern, simply appears to be a kind of folk alliterative device. (46)

From earliest colonial times, there has been a great deal of intermarriage between whites, blacks, and Indians, especially in the southeastern United States. However, according to Green, the black claim to Indian ancestry is "important, not because it has a genuine basis in reality, but rather because it has a purpose and intent separate from its basis in reality or fakery. . . . Because of the peculiar racial climate in which America was born, with a concern about the percentage or quantum of 'Indian blood' or 'Black blood,' . . . Indians and Blacks responded to that racial climate in many ways" (47).

Green argues that, at least prior to the Black Power movements of the 1960s, white "blood" was desirable for blacks (even allowing some to "pass for white"), but not for Indians ("half-breeds"). On the other hand, claiming Indian blood was a positive act for whites, so long as it did not imply negative consequences (47). Although Green believes that the most important function of assuming Indian identity is "cultural validation," she also notes that there can be a monetary payoff, although the role has seldom led either to "big money or big reputation" (48). She suggests a difference in the benefits of "cultural validation" by whites and blacks claiming Indian identity, with or without actual Indian ancestry. Anglo-Americans are "connecting to the America that existed before European invasion; . . . to both the real and to the primally mythic shaping of the country." Blacks, on the other hand, are perhaps "connecting to a world that allows them to be first, to be other than Black, other than white, other than victims that did not fight their enslavement" (48).

Although, as mentioned above, "wannabees" most often come in the form of a descendent of a Cherokee princess, I did hear one observation that Hispanic wannabees in California always claim to be Apaches. What is the general attitude among Indians toward wannabees? Usually, disdain and anger.

In her ethnography of the Indian community in Los Angeles, *Indian Country, L.A.: Maintaining Ethnic Community in Complex Society*, Joan Weibel-Orlando distinguishes between hobbyists, wannabees, "apple" Indians, and white people with "Indian hearts." Considering the enormous diversity among individuals in degree of Indian ancestry, multiple tribal ancestry, and acculturation in white and/or Indian society, these folk categories are certainly more evocative of "degree of Indianness" than any legal definition, including the one under scrutiny here. An apple Indian is an individual "who is phenotypically Indian but thinks in ways associated with the dominant culture," a category I have heard described as "red on the outside, white to the core"! A white person with an "Indian heart" is one "thought to have incorporated valued culture traits either through empathetic osmosis or from being inherently predisposed to such goodness of spirit" (Weibel-Orlando 207). This category includes people such as non-Indian spouses who have become true members of their Indian communities. Perhaps it also applies to individuals like the white artist certified as an artisan by the Yankton Sioux Tribe (see chapter 5). A "wannabee . . . self-consciously emulates Indian behavior and dress [and] conspicuously avows all things and causes Indian . . . [with] only a superficial understanding and appreciation of the subtleties of Indian world view, interactional style, and public presentation" (207).

Both wannabees and hobbyists frequent the Los Angeles Saturday night powwows. Weibel-Orlando characterizes these powwows as one of the important ethnic events that help make the community an example of Victor Turner's (1974) concept of *communitas*, whereby people in a society are bound together by the ritual fusion of the individual to the group. Hobbyists are whites who do not pretend to be Indian, but have a great admiration for Indian culture and often put considerable effort into researching costumes and mastering dances. They are, says Weibel-Orlando, more acceptable than wannabees because of their sincerity and lack of presumption. As to the attending wannabees, the author states that:

> "Wannabee" participation . . . is resented. "Wannabee" as a label has a decidedly negative connotation and is conferred on people who claim—often based on spurious documentation—that they are part-Indian. Their motives for doing so are thought to be less than sincere and probably gratuitous. Before powwow participation can function as a rite of incorporation into the ethnic community, other membership criteria must be met. Chief among these is a determination of the individual's personal motivation for seeking community incorporation. Demonstrated personal credentials

> such as community service, generosity, cooperativeness, and observable or verifiable Indian kin are other criteria for Indian community incorporation. People who, for economic or political reasons, suddenly opt for inclusion in Indian activities as a way of demonstrating ethnic group membership are suspect. This is especially true if they previously had preferred the company of non-Indians. (135–36)

The powwow wannabees can "expect to be treated with subtle yet complete civil inattention," meaning "avoidance behavior in public places" (150 n. 4).[1] In Los Angeles Indian events, this is "manifested by avoidance of eye contact and no attempt to speak to or interact with the offending individual, but no overt attempt to sanction the offending behavior in any way" (136, 150 n. 4).

Indian impostors are not confined to the arts or powwows. They particularly haunt the literary world and Hollywood filmmaking, and, indeed, several participants in the forums expressed a desire for the Indian Arts and Crafts Act to be expanded to cover the performing arts. Also, apparently some individuals can be exposed as non-Indian in one context and go to another area and continue their chosen role or even brazenly remain on the local scene being "Indian" (Atlatl 1992). Some forum participants described the situation where, on college campuses, both students (for scholarships) and faculty (to take advantage of the quest for cultural diversity) have fraudulently claimed Indian identity (Atlatl 1992; Thomas Jefferson Center 1993).

Some of the wannabees, according to one panelist, are leftovers from the Northwest fishing rights struggles of the 1960s. A number of the civil rights advocates of that time were welcomed in that struggle, but some of those "we still haven't shaken off; some simply stayed around as Indian people when they are not" (Atlatl 1992).

Wannabee artists, in addition to the purely fraudulent dealers in counterfeit Indian arts and crafts, are the intended targets of Pub. L. 101-644. What damage do they do? Most obviously, they siphon off money from the legitimate Indian arts and crafts market and damage its credibility, resulting in a loss of consumer confidence. The Commerce Department report demonstrates the considerable economic impact from the imported imitation goods. But for what I call "fake Indians," as distinguished from "fake goods," the considerations are a little different. The "fake Indians" are admittedly less of an economic problem, but their deception seems to be more of a personal affront than that of nameless and faceless foreign workers. Because the alleged impostors and tribal artists compete together and are personally known to one another, there is heightened opportunity for personal acrimony. Said one Indian artist (U.S. Department of the Interior, 1991 files):

> Too long have I observed and yes, voiced my outrage over the non-Indian who pushes and elbows the real Indian artist out of Indian art shows, galleries, museums and historical places. Many of these silver, forked-tongued non-Indians, and most of us know who they are, have risen to artistic prominence through fraudulently representing themselves as Indian artists. They have cared not one whit about our Indian culture, our tribal traditions, nor our respect for things dear to us in the Indian world. These frauds have only one objective and that is to make money.

Also, the artwork of "fake Indian" artists apparently falls more into the fine art category, where it can, or should, stand on its own merit. Pseudo-Indians also cause harm in all areas of endeavor by speaking to the non-Indian public with the voice of presumed authority on Indian culture.

How were the attitudes about wannabee artists expressed by the participants in the forums? A repeated refrain went something like this: These individuals are "ripping off the Indian communities"; "this is 1988, not 1492—they're not welcome to everything we have any longer; and they can't have our identity as a marketable commodity" (Atlatl 1992). Indians must "draw the line" and not let non-Indians take the "one last thing [they] can still steal" and market, the Indian "culture and identity" (Atlatl 1992). Another expression of this perception: "People typically show up in their thirties, always in connection with a per capita payment or career advancement" or for other monetary gain, but they don't come to "join us in poverty." In fact, the individual last quoted believes that the Indian Arts and Crafts Act is much too lenient and allows in a lot of "phonies" (Atlatl 1992). Wannabees, said another participant, are tolerated only because "we sell our art on white man's land" subject to laws of the dominant society, but no wannabees would be "prancing around on Indian land" because "we would do away with that real quick" (Atlatl 1992).

A telling example was provided by *Business Week*, which published a story, prior to the enactment of Pub. L. 101-644, about the New Mexico statute similar to the federal one (Atchison 1988: 71.) The article profiled sculptor "John F.", who claims to be one-fourth Indian, who "follow[s] the way of earth mother and sky father" and says, "in everything I do, I am Indian." In addition to other claimed Indian attributes, such as membership in the "intertribal Redtail Hawk Society," John F. claims to be "the official pipe maker of the Cheyenne-Arapaho tribe in Oklahoma." Not so, according to a representative of the Native American Artists Association, formed for the purpose of exposing artists "masquerading as Indians," who flatly said: "He is absolutely not an American Indian" (Atchison 1988: 71). One of the forum participants, a member of the Cheyenne-Arapaho Tribe, agreed and stated that not only was he not of Cheyenne ancestry, but that that tribe has no such thing as an "official pipemaker" (Atlatl 1992).

The considerations applicable to nontribal persons with Indian ancestry are, of course, different than with the wannabees. A logical case can be made that the tribal experience—the collective experience—is the essence of being Indian in this modern world. There are, as we have seen, tribes that function as such in the sociocultural sense, even if they are not recognized by the federal government as sovereign political entities. They include the terminated tribes and, perhaps, some of the not-yet-recognized groups. The American Indian experience, however, also includes people who, *because they were Indian*, were separated from the tribal context. In addition to those who chose to avoid government rolls, there were significant dislocations created by the federal government through policies that encouraged adoption of Indian children by whites and relocation of rural Indians to the cities. These circumstances raise the question of to what extent, and by which criteria, are these individuals and their descendants, raised in a nontribal environment, Indians or Americans of Indian descent.

According to Weibel-Orlando (1991: 1–2), as of 1980, there were approximately fifty thousand American Indians in Los Angeles, the largest urban Indian population in the United States, but a population that constitutes only a small ethnic and racial group compared to Los Angeles's other major ethnic and racial groups. The Los Angeles Indians are "characterized by extreme cultural heterogeneity, a dispersed settlement pattern, and scattered locations or nodes of symbolic and instrumental interaction" (2). Nevertheless, the "viability, tenacity, and political power" they exhibit causes the author to reject "existing analytic models of community" and develop an "anthropological model that adequately addresses the issue of nontraditional forms of community" (2). Weibel-Orlando characterizes the nature of such a community as follows:

> The social entity that substantial numbers of Indians in Los Angeles think of as their community is both a cognitive construct and an interactional pattern. Community can reside in the mind, reflect a sentiment, and be the product of symbolic as well as pragmatic social interactions unrestricted by considerations of shared space. . . .
>
> Today, the Los Angeles Indian community structure is sustained by a network of and intersecting participation in an impressive array of institutionalized political, economic, medical, religious, educational, recreational, and informational organizations, all of which are based on pragmatic but fragile constructions of ethnic unity. . . . [Groups] are recognized by both members and observers as the social structures that provide a continuing sense of history, community, and ethnic identity (traditional and novel) for those Indians who have chosen to "have a foot in both worlds" and to try "making it" in the city. (2, 4)

Weibel-Orlando describes some of the community events as "social dramas" (see Turner 1974), and explains that the "social and ritual behavior for which they are the contexts are a syncretic mix of cultural continuities and innovation" (5). The existence of the Los Angeles ethnic community depends upon a "critical mass" of individuals who choose to associate with other Indians even though they come from diverse backgrounds and from all parts of the country (5). The author, in 1986, distinguished over 150 "discrete, multiple, or sub-tribal specifications," noted the tendency of urban Indians to marry spouses of different tribal or ethnic groups, and further noted that there are families who relocated to Los Angeles in the 1930s and 1940s and represent four generations of city residents (21, 34). Yet out of this diversity of background has come an authentically Indian ethnic community:

> All of the usual markers, the whole cloth of community (common territory, mutually intelligible language, and shared ethos) appear, at first glance, to be missing in the Los Angeles Indian community. Yet its members have created a negotiated community. Choosing to ignore or to suspend the salience of ethnic markers that would have been divisive, Los Angeles Indians underscore and make salient those notions of traditional Indian ethos and lifeways that a critical mass of its members agree are shared pantribal traits and values. Community building has been a kind of cultural patchwork, . . . a highly creative and dynamic endeavor. (Weibel-Orlando 1991: 7–8)

The author compares the different levels of intraethnic and extraethnic categories to the segmented lineages of the Nuer (see Evans-Pritchard 1940) where the "boundaries of contrasting social categories and the criteria by which they are defined expand and contract in response to situational factors" (38). She describes many of these ethnic categories, such as Indian versus non-Indian, full-bloods versus mixed-bloods, traditionalists versus progressives, religious traditionalists versus Christian versus followers of syncretic religions, and urban versus rural reservation background, all of which are crosscut by the categories of subtribal, tribal, and regional cleavages. She concludes that, in the case of the Los Angeles Indian community, "ethnicity has come to mean a created supratribal identity and pan-Indian stance *vis à vis* the dominant society" (61). Although Weibel-

Orlando does not specifically mention the enrolled versus nonenrolled status, she notes that many individuals return frequently to their tribes and that "tribal pedigree is still highly weighted when determining who is or is not Indian, regardless of early socialization experiences that may have mitigated or ensured assumption of a tribal ethos" (40).

Another presumed source of Indian ethnicity and identity is found in the cultural aspects of the mainly political pan-Indian movement. Since the 1930s, many pan-Indian groups formed to present a more united political front in concerns of interest to American Indians in general. But the associated generation of generic Indian values, customs, and traits has been controversial and is seen by some as a threat to traditional tribal values and to represent the interests of "mixed-bloods and assimilated Native Americans who have surrendered much of their tribal identities" (Olson and Wilson 1984: 190–91). These generalized pan-Indian traits are present in at least two contexts significant for the question of Indian identity. For completely assimilated nontribal Indians or part-Indians, their acquisition may represent the only ethnic content available on which to model themselves as Indians. The second context is the adoption of these traits by groups such as the state-recognized tribes that have lost their Indian culture, a way to reconstitute cultural content. Unfortunately, adopting pan-Indian traits is a means for charlatan groups who claim to be Indian to present themselves as Indian. The pan-Indian traits show up most visibly in the adoption of the powwows and dancing. For example, Lerch describes the Waccamaw powwow (North Carolina), an important community event that includes the choosing of a princess and features dances and costumes of a pan-Indian style similar to Plains styles (1992: 70). These activities, even if based on nonlocal cultural traits, are meant to show and strengthen the Waccamaws' commitment to their heritage. "The symbols adopted may be pan-Indian and the regalia of Plains origin, but the Indian identity being celebrated is local" (71). Nagel points out that cultural renewal involves both cultural construction and reconstruction, processes that include not only cultural revivals, restorations, and revisions, but also innovations (1996: 46–47). Borrowing is one source of innovation.

According to David C., enrolled Cherokee genealogist, the Indian impersonators first became a problem in the 1930s by "pass[ing] off as Indian art the generic pan-Indian painting so prevalent among the non-member artists" (U.S. Department of the Interior, 1991 files). Concerning these "impersonators," he says that:

> the non-member artist[s] all give the same tired old rhetoric about their Indian ancestors. To the untrained, their woeful tales sound so pitiful, they just have to be true. The sad truth is, their tales are not true and do not stand up to honest diligent scrutiny. Some of their stories include: my ancestors jumped off the trail of tears in Illinois, my ancestors were from Kentucky, . . . all of my records burned up in a court house in Arkansas, my great-grandmother was a full blood Cherokee princess (the Cherokees had no royalty and where were all the bucks?), and on and on.

Who is to say what is authentic or not in terms of Indian experience? An analogy of the "authenticity" of one's background can be made to the "authenticity" of the content of "Indian" artwork. George C. Longfish and Joan Randall (1988) write about the expectations of nonartist professionals who express concern over the content of Indian art. They suggest that these people, which include art historians, anthropologists, and critics, are not interested in "the quality of the art or whether or not the artist is truly an

Indian," but whether the work is traditional, therefore ostensibly more Indian than work with no recognizable imagery or with familiar symbols but presented in nontraditional ways. The authors argue that because Indian artists "do not allow superficial contradictions of their different Indian realities to limit their creativity," then "the issue of authenticity is a problem for the non-artist professionals to solve, not the artists" (22–23). The imagery of traditional style "has come to be equated with all Indian art," thus the frequency of questions at exhibits asking where the rugs and pottery are—"the viewers are not satisfied unless they see the 'real' Southwest" (23). Unfortunately, the departure from the traditional is too often interpreted by these professionals as "assimilation or 'merging into the mainstream'" rather than as a reflection of a "growing and changing . . . culture" (21). Because Indian artists live in both the traditional and modern worlds, "the contradictions of Indian territory are authentically Indian" (24).

Other contradictions inherent in Indian existence include the formation of an urban ethnic identity; the experiences of those state groups, recognized or not, that do have a legitimate claim to Indianness; and the terminated tribes. The nonenrolled individuals would surely argue that these and other disenfranchising experiences, such as adoption into white families, relocation, and hiding out from removal are equally authentic Indian experiences. With artwork itself, there seems to be a pronounced tendency to equate real or authentic with traditional, and traditional with aboriginal.

American Indian identity is truly a demographer's nightmare. About the only thing clear is that it has always been in a process of change and will continue to change, not only because it is a social construct, but also because the social facts upon which the identity itself is based are not static. Snipp (1989: 310–11) suggests that two distinct populations are being created today. One consists of "individuals strongly connected to their American Indian heritage, [which] in terms of their residence, lifestyle, socioeconomic characteristics, and even appearance" is "easily identifiable as American Indian." The other is composed of those "who can recall, legitimately, some amount of Indian ancestry but have little knowledge of Indian culture and in most respects do not resemble the core population of American Indians." He predicts that the population growth will be fastest in the second category (1989: 310–11).

In the next chapter, I will describe some specific situations relative to Pub. L. 101-644 concerning the problematic issue of identity.

Chapter 5

"REAL" INDIANS

Certification as an "Indian Artisan"

The entire concept of the certification process is new territory. As noted before, the federal legislators who drafted the Indian Arts and Crafts Act perceived a need to broaden the definition of "Indian" beyond the requirement of membership in a federally recognized tribe. Curiously, they did not just add a provision with a minimum degree of blood quantum requirement, as has been used in numerous statutes. Although that approach would not overcome the basic problems of the statute, it is at least familiar and works in other contexts. Then Congressman Campbell's aide stated that this provision was drafted with the help of the Department of Justice and was intended to be consistent with *Santa Clara Pueblo v. Martinez*, the case that recognized the right of a tribe to determine its own membership (Public Forum 1991). The lineage requirement is the only regulatory guideline concerning tribal authority or obligation to offer certification. The Department of the Interior, Solicitor-Indian Affairs, issued an opinion (which is not binding on any court) on April 23, 1993, concerning certification (U.S. Department of the Interior 1993). It concludes that, taking the legislative history of the statute into consideration, Congress's intent was to authorize certification only of artisans "of the tribe's lineage." It also notes that this raises the problem of the criteria to be used by state-recognized tribes for determining membership and that of both state- and federally recognized tribes for certification.

The question concerning certification of an individual with no Indian ancestry is not hypothetical. At least two tribes have already certified such artisans, not waiting for the final regulations to be written. The subsequently written regulations do require certified artisans to be of the lineage of a tribal member. They also reiterate the statutory prohibition against charging a fee to prevent such action by any tribe that might be tempted to do so purely to generate revenue. We can thus assume that such certifications reflect other than financial motivations.

By Resolution 92-68, passed on June 4, 1992, the federally recognized Yankton Sioux Tribe of South Dakota certified Chad N., who was not Indian by blood, as a "Tribal Artist according to the rules and regulations of the Indian Arts and Crafts Act of 1990" (U.S. Department of the Interior, 1992 files). Someone challenging this will no doubt point out that he is certified as a "tribal" rather than as an "Indian" artist, but that is easily corrected. The body of the resolution states that the Yankton Sioux tribe has the right to recognize "any enrolled members and/or any extended family nonenrolled members as Tribal Artists." Chad N. writes that he was adopted by a traditional family on the reservation, practices the traditional culture, and speaks the language:

> As an adolescent, Chad was adopted by Dakota historian Joseph Rockboy, and began learning the language, philosophy, tradition and culture of the Ehanhktujnwan Dakota (Yankton Sioux). In 1972 he began his twelve year appren-

> ticeship to his uncle and benefactor, internationally known Dakota bead artist, Clarence Rockboy.
>
> Chad's work primarily has focused on creating articles for use in traditional ceremonies. The articles he has produced are being used by traditional peoples of many different tribes. (U.S. Department of the Interior, 1992 files)

The federally recognized Tonkawa Tribe of Oklahoma, through its Tribal Business Committee, passed Resolution T-SR-02-2 on December 18, 1992, certifying Bill R. as an "Indian Artisan of the Tonkawa Tribe of Oklahoma" (U.S. Department of the Interior, 1993 files). At least two objections were made to the Indian Arts and Crafts Association complaining that artist Bill R. was non-Indian (U.S. Department of the Interior, 1993 files). The association replied that, inasmuch as its criteria for membership track the federal arts and crafts law, such certification is sufficient for membership (U.S. Department of the Interior, 1993 files). The Sault Ste. Marie Tribe of Chippewa Indians (Michigan) expressed support for the federal law and interest in adopting a certification procedure. In a letter to the Arts and Crafts Board, the tribal chairman indicated that they were not opposed to the certification of non-Indian artists who "produce 'Indian' art that is authentic, genuine and not opposable to any tribal group" if such individuals are "pursuing a traditional native American way of life or at least have a very good understanding of native tradition." This letter also warned of the possibility of misuse of the certification process by nontribal artists who "manufacture Indian art for mass consumption . . . [because] mass production of Indian art has little if anything to do with the spiritual and traditional values of Indian people" (U.S. Department of the Interior, 1993 files).

Another problem inherent in the certification solution is illustrated by the case of the late Willard Stone, who claimed

Cherokee ancestry. He was a well-known sculptor and his depiction of the Trail of Tears is the logo for the Cherokee National Historical Society (Oklahoma). Apparently, some Cherokees believe that he should be certified posthumously by the tribe as an Indian artisan; others disagree on the grounds that it would set a precedent which would make it difficult to deny certification to other artists (*McAlester (Okla.) News-Capital and Democrat* 1990). His family carries on the fight, both on his behalf and that of his niece, artist Jeanne R.

THE CHEROKEES OF OKLAHOMA

Issues concerning the identity of American Indian artists troubled the Cherokee Nation in Oklahoma for some time before the enactment of Pub. L. 101-644 and, indeed, contributed to the perceived need for such a statute. Oklahoma, like several other states with a significant American Indian population, has a state arts and crafts sales act, enacted in 1974 (American Indian Arts and Crafts Act of 1974, 78 Oklahoma Statutes 71 *et seq.*). The Oklahoman Cherokees' uncomfortable position in the forefront of this dispute owes much to their large population—approximately ninety thousand—and to their particular criterion for membership which, in light of their history, is almost guaranteed to create disgruntlement among nonmembers who nevertheless claim Cherokee ancestry. The sole criterion for membership in the Cherokee Nation of Oklahoma is proof of descent from an individual listed on the Dawes Commission Rolls. No minimum blood quantum is required, meaning that with each generation some members become less and less biologically Indian (Thornton 1990: 140).

The Dawes Commission was formed in the late 1800s to carry out the allotment mandate of the General Allotment

Act of 1887 (the Dawes Act). The Dawes Act exempted eastern Indian Territory (now Oklahoman) tribes, but they were subjected to allotment by subsequent statutes. The Dawes Commission was actually a series of commissions whose members went out into the field and conducted surveys of Indian populations as a basis for the intended allotments. Thus, for those tribes subjected to the survey, there was actually a series of rolls. The Creeks in Indian Territory, for example, had five different enrollment periods. In Indian Territory, the rolls for the Five Civilized Tribes (Cherokee, Creek, Chickasaw, Choctaw, and Seminole) were open between 1886 and 1914 (Debo 1940: 37, 47). Like many acts designed to "help" American Indians, allotment was intended to overcome the perceived limitations to progress of the communal system of landholding. As Senator Dawes put it, "There is no selfishness, which is at the bottom of civilization" (22). However, many individuals of the Five Civilized Tribes could not, or would not, sign the Rolls; this included many of the more traditional groups. On the other hand, many unscrupulous non-Indians tried to get in on the land allotment by moving to Indian territory and claiming Indian identity. According to Angie Debo, some of the non-Indians illegally intruding into the Indian territory "advanced some fantastic claim to citizenship, and . . . loudly demanded every privilege enjoyed by the Indians in spite of repeated denials of their claims by the tribal authorities" (12). As Anders describes the situation, "When the news of free land hit the local newspapers, the Dawes Commission was flooded with thousands of applications from people claiming tribal citizenship" (1992: 87).

Despite the tribes' objections to the interlopers, "the Supreme Court upheld the authority of the Dawes Commission to make the rolls, and they were compelled to acquiesce" (Debo 1940: 36). The official tribal rolls and censuses were not in good order because "the recognition of citizenship rested more on family and neighborhood knowledge than upon official registration," and there were instances of manipulation by tribal officials for their own purposes (37). Not only were the "Conservative fullbloods . . . extremely reluctant to enroll," but, in addition, the commissioners were "besieged by white and Negro claimants, usually prompted by scheming attorneys who were determined to share in the tribal property" (37). In one distribution alone, the commission "awarded allotments to over 41,000 people—even though the Cherokee tribal census of 1890 listed only 22,015 enrolled members" (Anders 1992: 88). Another commission, appointed later by the president of the United States to look into the many cases that ended up in litigation, "uncovered a great mass of nauseous evidence, and rejected a large number of claims upon the ground that they had been advanced through perjury and forgery" (Debo 1940: 39). Finally, in addition to these fraudulent interlopers, the Cherokee had themselves admitted to citizenship during the 1800s some non-Indians.

These developments mean that not only can an Oklahoman Cherokee be of minimal Indian ancestry, he or she can be without any Indian ancestry at all, because "descendants of all those appearing on the Dawes Commission rolls—including blacks and whites—are eligible for membership in the Cherokee Nation of Oklahoma" (Thornton 1990: 139–40).

Former Cherokee Principal Chief Wilma Mankiller is sympathetic to the plight of the descendants of those left off of the Dawes roll, which she characterizes as a "tool of oppression," and who therefore are not eligible for membership: "An Indian is an Indian regardless of the degree of

Indian blood or which little government card they do or do not possess" (quoted in Hales 1990b: 3A). This sympathy backfired politically when, early in her term, she honored her predecessor's policy of issuing letters to nonmembers of Cherokee descent, vouching for their Cherokee ancestry (Mankiller 1990: 7A). Interestingly, a number of photocopies of those letters with different names, presumably substituted, have been sent to the Arts and Crafts Board.

Chief Mankiller wrote in a guest column in a local Oklahoma newspaper that she deplored the acrimony that has proven to be destructive to the legitimate debate. She noted that there were only about a half-dozen nonenrolled Cherokee artists recognized by the Cherokee Nation, including the Willard Stone family, and chastised one of the more vocal critics. "There are those taking the absolute position that artists who enter Indian art shows must be members of a federally-recognized tribe. One of these . . . is an artist himself, a 1/64th degree Cherokee who has been a member of the Cherokee Nation for only two years. Prior to that time, he entered several Indian art shows. . . . Now, he is attempting to prevent others from doing the same" (1990: 7a).

Chief Mankiller, however, is less charitable to various groups in several states who claim to be Cherokee. In a letter sent to various state governors in January 1992 (see chapter 3), she noted that "over forty-six . . . different Cherokee groups in twenty . . . states including Oklahoma . . . claim existence as Indian tribes," representative of the "onslaught of those who would have themselves similarly recognized but are neither eligible for recognition by the tribe nor the federal government." She warned the governors that these groups, who have little hope of obtaining federal recognition, seek state recognition as a perceived first step toward the ultimate goal of federal recognition. She cited the confusion these groups cause with their official seals, membership cards, and the like, and requested that state officials refrain from granting state recognition to any group that does not first obtain federal recognition, thus meeting the latter's strict requirements. She appended to the letter a "preliminary" list of thirty-nine entities using the Cherokee name, located in seventeen states, including faraway Vermont and Oregon.[1] Several of those groups have indeed been recognized by their state governments.

Recent events, but that predate Pub L. 101-644, illustrate the Cherokee difficulty.[2] During the 1989 Cherokee National Holiday, enrolled Cherokee artist John G. challenged the inclusion of the works of Troy A., a nonenrolled artist who claims Cherokee ancestry. Again, at the 1990 Holiday, artist John G., joined by enrolled genealogist David C., challenged a promotion by the Seven Clans Trading Company (funded by a federal grant to the Cherokee Nation) of several nonenrolled artists. Two of the featured artists were Jeanne R., niece of the late sculptor Willard Stone, and Cherokee Master Artist Bert S. The "Cherokee Master Artist" designation is made by the Five Civilized Tribes Museum in Muskogee, Oklahoma. Thus is suggested the anomaly of a non-Cherokee Cherokee Master Artist (Hales 1990a: 1A). There are apparently several nonenrolled Cherokee Master Artists.

Such challenges invoked the Oklahoma American Indian Arts and Crafts Sales Act of 1974, which defines "Indian" as a person enrolled or a lineal descendent of a person enrolled in a recognized Indian tribe, band, or pueblo, or on a U.S. Bureau of Indian Affairs enrollment listing. The Oklahoma statute thus also defines an Indian in political terms. A nonenrolled Cherokee attorney is quoted as stating that he knows of an individual full-blood who is not eligible for Cherokee membership and is therefore not an Indian under the Oklahoma law, but "I'd have to get a Cherokee interpreter to try to explain to him that he's considered white" (Hales 1990b).

Passage of the federal Indian Arts and Crafts Act of 1990, in December of that year, added fuel to this long-smoldering debate. Uncertain of their position, the directors of two Indian museums in eastern Oklahoma—the Five Civilized Tribes Museum and the Cherokee Cultural Heritage Center—closed them down, although they reopened them shortly thereafter (*McAlester (Okla.) News-Capital and Democrat* 1990: 1A). These and other museums, in the absence of regulations, have experimented with the use of a "Non-Government Enrolled Descendant" (NGED) designation, apparently at the suggestion of the Willard Stone family (U.S. Department of the Interior, 1991 files).

One particularly interesting difference in perspective between some tribal and nontribal Indians has emerged in the context of Pub. L. 101-644. It is the feeling among some tribal members that unless individuals actively seek association with their tribes they should not capitalize on an Indian identity. This is especially marked in the Oklahoman Cherokee art community because of the considerable number of Cherokees who did not appear on the Dawes Roll, including some of the most traditional and conservative families, who viewed the commission with suspicion. Those contemporary artists who claim to be descendants of these families characterize that stance as integrity in the face of the enemy; some tribal members see it as desertion.

Following are statements made by proponents of both views in the context of their differences about the Indian Arts and Crafts Act. I have also included statements by non-

Cherokees on this issue of the sincerity of individuals who retain their "heritage" but reject their tribe. This attitude is not limited to the Cherokees, but is more or less pan-Indian.

The first examples are statements from nonenrolled individuals who claim Indian descent. Susan T. states that she is of one-eighth Indian descent and is a wildlife artist who has recently begun to paint Indian subjects and wants to market herself as an Indian artist. She claims that her father is one-fourth Cherokee, but that he was put into an orphanage and that family connections were lost.

> There are—as you may well know—many—many artists in my situation. I understand the Act was enacted to protect Indian markets from an infiltration from Hong Kong and Korea. . . .
>
> However—I don't believe the act was meant to affect people like me. I am an artist who does all original art work—one can tell by looking at me that I am Indian. But I have lost my documentation through [*sic*] ancestors. Actually, until now, because it is a stumbling block in my Art Career, I or my father never felt a need for documentation. We just always knew we were Indian. . . .
>
> . . . Please consider artists like myself—and allow us to continue our careers. We are honest—hardworking people who just want to go to our shows and sell our art. (U.S. Department of the Interior, files [n.d.])

Jeanne R. is an artist who claims Cherokee descent and is the niece of noted sculptor Willard Stone, now deceased. She states:

> Both my mother and father are descended from two of the many Indian families who refused the mark of the government. The legacy I received from my ancestors was not denial of my heritage, but distrust of "government aid." I almost have to thank this new bill for truly opening my eyes.

> I now have a better understanding of what my people gave to me—they gave me independence. (U.S. Department of the Interior, 1990 files)

John M., an Oklahoman who creates pyrographic art, a woodburning technique, identifies himself as a Choctaw who has been recommended for Master Cherokee Artist. The following statement was submitted for the forum in Oklahoma City: "Here is your chance to refuse to punish an Indian just because his fore-fathers were strong-willed and refused to be put on the rolls and to be put into the white man's camps" (Public Forum 1991).

The following statements reflect the opposite view, one held by some, although not all, tribal members. Mavis D., an enrolled Cherokee, was appointed by Chief Mankiller to the Cherokee Arts and Crafts Advisory Board, but expressed her opinion only as a personal one:

> Any person who wishes to receive a benefit because of their claim of American Indian ancestry should be required to show that they merit this benefit. Only those whose families have held on to their ancestral culture in the face of the constant and bitter oppression of the majority should be allowed to reap the rewards of this culture now that its spirit and beauty are finally accepted in our society. Those who are registered tribal members can conclusively demonstrate by the fact of this membership that their ancestors were proud to be Indians. (Public Forum 1991)

Deborah A., editor of *Feather Review News*, describes herself as a Kiowa artist. "The artists 'screaming' the loudest over the passage of P.L. 101-644 . . . are those who cannot prove membership in any tribe. Most Indians who are really interested in their heritage will make some attempt to enroll with their tribe (U.S. Department of the Interior, 1991 files).

Genealogist and enrolled Cherokee David C. expounds a little on this:

> In 1936, it suddenly became a source of pride to be Indian, at least that is how it appeared to the outside world. A pride that could not be destroyed lived in the hearts of the tribal members who, in spite of the adversity of being Indian when it wasn't popular and even knowing that they could be killed for openly claiming it, stayed with the tribe, enrolled when required to and otherwise lived an Indian life. The non-member artists, if their ancestors ever were Indians, were ashamed, hid among the whites and participated in the oppression of the tribal Indians. Now they want to come back to the tribe and expect us to welcome them. I say no! . . . If their ancestors ever really were Cherokee or even Indian, it is not legitimate to come back to the tribe now, after an absence of over 150 years and try to take advantage of what we had built. (U.S. Department of the Interior, 1991 files)

The situation of Jeanne R., quoted above, attracted the interest of the Thomas Jefferson Center for the Protection of Free Expression, headquartered in Charlottesville, Virginia, an institution with informal ties to the University of Virginia. The center's stated mission is to defend free expression in its broadest meaning. This organization sponsored a meeting held on June 22, 1993, in the United States Capitol Building, for the purpose of bringing together persons with different perspectives on these issues. In addition to Ms. R., present were several congressional aides and representatives from the Thomas Jefferson Center, the Indian Arts and Crafts Board, and the National Museum of the American Indian. Other participants included several knowledgeable American Indian individuals with varying points of view. These included a prominent attorney, a well-known activist-lobbyist (also quoted in the context of other forums), and several artists and craftspeople. The meeting was quite lively, the discussion occasionally heated.

In its written summation of this event,[3] the center made the following observations, here further summarized. All participants agreed that (1) individuals and businesses try to "cash in" on the art market, and thus there is a need to protect consumers and "legitimate" artists; (2) there are individuals of Indian heritage who are not enrolled and, for various reasons, cannot be certified; (3) the act has created uncertainty among gallery owners and artists as to their positions; (4) "the issue of tribal enrollment . . . seems to reach well beyond the arts community and the Act"; and (5) "participants agreed on the need for more face-to-face practical discussion . . . and several warned that the intensity of debate over the Act is driving a dangerous wedge between normally like-minded Native Americans."

The center's report stated that the arguments made in support of the act were (1) the intent to prevent the threat to the Indian art market from misrepresentation, (2) the great importance of tribal determination of membership, and (3) that Indian status is a legal distinction, not a racial classification. The report further stated as views of supporters of the act (1) that nonenrolled individuals of American Indian descent should seek a relationship with their tribes, (2) that a clear definition of Indian status is needed, and (3) that they see no First Amendment problems since the act is not about prohibiting sales of art works, but actually deals with the question of tribal sovereignty.

Arguments against the act, according to the center, included (1) that the certification requirement excludes the many artists of Indian heritage who cannot obtain certification for many reasons, such as belonging to terminated tribes, having been adopted, or being of descent that does not meet the particular tribe's enrollment criteria; (2) that art galleries may shy away from selling works by Indian artists; (3) that the certification option may be unsatisfactory and discriminatory; and (4) that the statute does violate their First Amendment rights and that artists other than Indians do not have to document their heritage in order to sell their work.

What the center's report does not convey are the strong feelings behind the opinions expressed. As an observer, I witnessed the frustration of Jeanne R., who believes the act excludes legitimate Indian artists; anger by the western artist who feels the act has "devastated us as a people"; impatience by those who insist that only a tribe can determine who is an Indian; annoyance at the "infiltration of every area of our tribal life" by non-Indians; and disgust at "white people telling Indians who Indians are."

The foregoing discussion of the problem of the Cherokee Nation of Oklahoma, a federally recognized tribe, and nonenrolled individuals who have, or claim to have, Cherokee ancestry, illustrates one type of boundary that Pub. L. 101-644 has drawn to mark Indians off from non-Indians. That boundary distinguishes between enrolled or certified and nonenrolled individuals, regardless of the presence or absence of sociocultural and/or biological ancestral attributes. The following example is another kind of boundary drawing—one that focuses on groups whose Indianness is questioned. Although the group chosen is within the act's scope because it is state-recognized, it nonetheless illustrates the difficulties of seeking state or federal recognition.

THE LUMBEE OF NORTH CAROLINA

Although each state-recognized tribe is unique in its makeup and history, a brief look at the problematical Lumbee Tribe of North Carolina may be helpful. Although its members apparently do have considerable Indian ancestry, the question remains, Are they an Indian "tribe" or a group of interrelated families with some Indian ancestry and a collective self-identification as Indian, and are those the same thing? The Lumbees, mentioned in chapter 3, are state-recognized, and thus will be included as Indians for the purposes of the Indian Arts and Crafts Act, but their predicament concerning federal recognition illustrates one of the types of arbitrariness I suggest, namely arbitrariness of process. By that, I do not mean the administrative acknowledgement process, but the overall working of federal law, as shown by this example.

The Lumbees are a large group, some forty thousand in population, and have been studied quite thoroughly. Blu, in *The Lumbee Problem: The Making of an American Indian People* (1980), examines their history in the context of southern race consciousness and traces their transition from "free persons of color" or "free Negroes" in the 1700s to their current status as a state-recognized tribe and one with a unique type of federal recognition, or nonrecognition according to how one interprets it.

The Lumbees' state recognition dates from 1885. The group unsuccessfully sought federal recognition through federal legislation in 1888, 1899, 1910, 1912, 1924, 1932, and 1933 (U.S. Senate 1991b: 6–7). The federal statute in question (the Lumbee Act of June 7, 1956 [70 Stat. 254]) was passed in 1956; its wording followed that of the state recognition statute but specifically excluded the Lumbees from eligibility for federal services provided by the Bureau of Indian Affairs. Two other tribes subject to this type of quasi-recognition, the Ysleta del Sur Pueblo (Texas) and the Pascua Yaqui Tribe (Arizona), have since been granted full recognition by special federal legislation (U.S. Senate 1991b:

10). The 1956 Lumbee statute is subject to different interpretations, including whether or not it constituted de facto federal recognition of the Lumbees. The Lumbees applied to the Bureau of Acknowledgment and Research for administrative recognition under 25 C.F.R. § 83, but are now considered barred from that avenue because the 1956 act specifically forbade eligibility for federal services; therefore, remedial legislation is required. In the 1970s, groups of Lumbees began calling themselves the Tuscarora and sought federal recognition under that banner, but were equally unsuccessful (Sider 1993: 3–4). In 1989, the Lumbees' representative, Congressman Charles Rose, introduced a bill to have the group fully recognized; a similar bill was introduced in the Senate. The House bill was considered by the Committee on Interior and Insular Affairs, but died there. The Lumbees are currently listed by the Bureau of Acknowledgment and Research as six different groups containing the tribal names Lumbee, Tuscarora (two groups), Hatteras Tuscarora, and Cherokee (two groups) (U.S. Department of the Interior 1996).

These people have been documented as living in Robeson County since at least 1790 (Blu 1980: 39). They apparently have white, black, and Indian ancestry, and their origins are uncertain, an impediment to social acceptance and federal recognition as Indians. They demonstrate no evidence of having retained any aboriginal culture traits, and they are part of, not apart from, the larger society. Yet Blu finds their "Indianness" to have both external and internal elements keyed to a "basic group identity" that exists even in the absence of cultural differences or political organization (1). She characterizes their political behavior over time as a positive "we Indian" drive as well as a distancing from earlier identification as nonwhite or black (133).

The Lumbees, who take their name from the nearby Lumber River, claim descent from survivors of Raleigh's Lost Colony of Roanoke and local Indians. They suggested this as a reason for the adoption of the English language and loss of other Indian cultural traits: "We never had tribal ways" (Blu 135). They have no reservation, but put great value on owning land in the county, which they consider a "homeland," and believe that the land should remain in Indian hands (163–68).

Blu suggests that their identity as Indians is expressed externally as "an articulate, well-formulated . . . explanation, an intellectual account of the origins of the group couched in terms that are meaningful to relevant outsiders" (134). By this, she means the Lost Colony account. The internal aspect is "inarticulately expressed and only loosely or ill-formulated, an often unselfconscious moral and emotional blueprint of 'who we are'" (134–35). This latter pattern shows up in behavioral characteristics that the Lumbees identify as Indian. The primary behaviors are pride; "meanness," not in the sense of pettiness, but of "standing up for one's self" or a "tendency to react violently" when insulted; and cohesiveness or "sticking together" (120–49). These behaviors, plus a Lumbee surname, speaking a distinctive dialect, residence in or near Robeson County, and physical appearance serve as their defining characteristics.

In her analysis, Blu examines some of the definitions and concepts in the literature concerning ethnicity (225). She challenges many of the accepted definitions and usages and concludes that "none of the features offered as defining characteristics of ethnicity or ethnic groups seems to be universally the case," and that many of the definitions can be, and are, applied to obviously nonethnic groups. She further suggests that the concept of ethnic group is useful only in the United States because it is generally understood and is not infused with notions of class consciousness. Ethnicity should not be used as an analytic tool, but seen as an "important form of social differentiation in the United States" (227). The "problem" of the Lumbee is "how differences among people are conceived, worked out, and changed over time," which in this case resulted in a change from race-based identity to ethnicity (201).

At the congressional committee hearing on the 1989 Lumbee Recognition Act, an impressive array of anthropologists and historians testified that, given the particular history and geography of the region, these people are almost certainly descended from a group of Cheraws who retired into the somewhat inaccessible swamps in the area, where they were joined by refugee groups and individuals from destroyed tribes. These witnesses included anthropologists William Sturtevant, Jack Campisi, Raymond Fogelson, and, indirectly through reference to his work from the 1930s, John Swanton. At the hearing, many other tribes put into the record statements to the effect that it is unfair to the tribes who are going through the rigorous federal acknowledgment process for a tribe to be recognized directly by Congress. The representative of the Branch of Acknowledgment and Research stated that a brief review of the Lumbee Tribe's petition showed areas that needed further documentation, and that the documents submitted did not support the link to the Cheraw tribe (U.S. Senate 1991b: 22–23).

The Lumbees are one of the groups categorized as triracial isolates, as discussed in chapter 3. Gerald M. Sider, however, argues that the Lumbees' difficulties with recognition are not due to racial admixture inasmuch as other Indian groups have successfully absorbed considerable numbers of people with non-Indian ancestry; some, such as the Seminoles, exhibit a great deal of black mixing (1993: xxii).

I have presented the Cherokee and Lumbee stories to illustrate two very different types of situations addressing the question, What is an Indian? With the Cherokee, the question focuses on those individuals outside of the group membership. With the Lumbee, it is the nature of the group itself that raises the question. I do not mean to suggest that either tribe is typical in any way of others similarly situated, just that these two basically different situations both exist, and both represent the types of context in which the Indian Arts and Crafts Act of 1990 will be litigated.

CONCLUSIONS

It is not my intention—or place—to comment on the *political* desirability of the Indian Arts and Crafts Act of 1990. Nor do I intend to suggest which criteria mark the boundary where Indian identity is abandoned or alienated. Some of the act's legal vulnerabilities have been mentioned briefly and others await conception in the minds of clever lawyers. I do suggest, however, that the statute is fatally flawed in a social sense, which I will make apparent.

From the forum discussions, I have abstracted several common themes evoked by the Indian Arts and Crafts Act. Although separated here for purposes of presentation, they are, in fact, different aspects of a whole. The only apparent structural differences are the tribal perspective, naturally expressed by tribal people, and the individual perspective of the nontribal individual artist excluded from proclaiming an Indian identity when marketing his or her arts and crafts. There is not, however, a strict dichotomy of tribal versus nontribal individuals expressing these perspectives, as evidenced by those tribal Indians who spoke of the value of including those who are not members of a tribe.

I

Sovereignty, explicit or implicit in all Indian law, was mentioned in the forum discussions in a number of contexts. Some instances were noted in the quotations in chapter 2. There appears to be near consensus that Pub. L. 101-644 affects, or has the potential to affect, American Indian sovereignty. There is no consensus on how. The act is seen variously as an agent for maintaining, expanding, or threatening that sovereignty, as evidenced by comments made at the 1992 Atlatl conference. The following are examples:

An Ojibway artist stated that he liked the "core concept" of Pub. L 101-644 because it "respects" sovereignty, and continued sovereignty "will enable us to survive for the next 500 years" and preserve the "land base and self-government" required to remain a "united cohesive nation" with its own "language and culture." But others viewed the act as just one more white man's law that "whittles away, piece by piece, bit by bit, Indian peoples." The Washington, D.C., activist-lobbyist quoted elsewhere argued that something of sovereignty has been lost in the law—"the standard that the Indian nations have sole discretionary authority regarding citizenry." An Indian Arts and Crafts Board commissioner, speaking personally as an artist, suggested that the statute expands the reach of sovereign power because it provides a tribe with another form of membership for nonmember individuals. Although he is an enrolled member of a tribe, he expressed concern about children who may not marry within the tribe or with kin who, for whatever reason, are excluded from membership. He saw this act, even if limited to artists and craftspeople, as going beyond criteria such as blood quantum and encompassing the criterion of "community recognition" in the "official" determination of the

"Who is an Indian?" question. He envisioned it as a spark to create more "community," because "we are a communal tribal people" and the "key word is *tribal*; . . . without that community we don't exist" except as individuals. He called upon those who are tribally enrolled and their tribal governments to help those disenfranchised tribes and individuals seeking inclusion.

Some, however, cautioned that the concepts of community and sovereignty be used with care because they may mean, as ideals, different things to different people or groups; that is, some may prefer a more inclusive effect, whereas more traditional groups may prefer to use them to exclude. Thornton cites a study conducted by Ronald Trosper in the 1970s that compared the different policies of tribes concerning inclusivity of membership (Thorton 1990: 142, citing Trosper 1976). Trosper, a member of the Confederated Salish and Kootenai Tribes of the Flathead Reservation (Montana), compared those tribes to the Cherokees in Oklahoma and North Carolina. The Salish-Kootenai are composed mainly of mixed-bloods and narrowly escaped termination in the 1950s. In 1960, they tightened the blood quantum requirement for membership and now require a minimum one-quarter. This promotion of blood quantum over community is characterized as an "entrenchment" necessary for tribal survival. The Cherokees, however, have remained inclusive, which is their policy for tribal survival. Their "large, dispersed mixed-blood population enabled them to achieve 'political power' as a tribe and to protect a 'core' of more full-blood, more traditional Cherokee" (Thornton 1990: 142–43). Thus, the very definition of Indian-as-citizen may owe as much to the strategy for political survival of the group as to any sociocultural criteria.

Another perspective on the Salish-Kootenai strategy is the perceived need to maintain a population of Indians who appear to be Indians:

> Rights to land and services originally based upon treaty commitments depend in fact upon stereotypes for survival. Congruence with the stereotypes must be preserved because Congress controls Indian property rights unchecked by Constitutional guarantees. . . . Should Indians appear to be like whites, valuable rights could be taken away by Congress in response to an argument that all American citizens are the "same." If accepted, this argument would classify special treaty rights as illegitimate "discrimination." Should Indian blood become thinned through intermarriage, the non-Indian appearing children of tribal members must be excluded in order to protect tribal existence. The dilemma arises because intermarriage under an exclusive racial definition of membership will gradually cause a tribe to die out. Tribal existence is threatened by either an inclusive or exclusive rule. (Trosper 1976: 257)

These comments echo the statement by the Hopi tribal chairman, quoted in chapter 2, that continued sovereignty depends upon Indians who look like Indians, live like Indians, and speak Native languages.

Another concern, closely related to and inherent in the sovereignty issue, is that of the tribe as a community, a collectivity. "Community" is not an adequate term, however. When American Indians say they are a "tribal people," the meaning I hear is what Deloria calls their sense of being "a people," a description frequently expressed. Deloria and Lytle write that "in the concept of the people we find both the psychological and the political keys that unlock the puzzling dilemma of the present and enable us to understand why American Indians view the world as they do today" (1984: 8). Deloria and Lytle's comment suggests the reason why treaties are held so sacred and alive even today. The treaties represent a "sacred pledge made by one people to another," to be honored as a matter of personal integrity rather than being dealt with as mere legal documents that are too often seen as fair game for circumvention. The "idea of the people is primarily a religious concept" (8). In a 1971 article entitled "Persistent Cultural Systems," anthropologist Edward Spicer (796) writes of the importance of the concept of "a people," which is "a determinable set of human individuals who believe in a given set of identity symbols." The persistence relies on a process of opposition, or conflict, between the "people" and the dominant society and not upon any particular cultural traits.

The political nature of the tribe-as-sovereign is the "tool" (as one speaker put it) that preserves the tribe-as-community in the larger sense of preserving "the people." Some of this perception has been indicated in prior recitations; tribe-as-sovereign cannot, in practice, be separated from tribe-as-community. As noted in chapter 2, the entire thrust of American Indian policy, until very recently, has been to promote the assimilation of Native peoples into the mainstream of American society. The tribal communities, using as best they could the often inadequate tool of the limited sovereignty recognized by the federal government, have managed to hold back to some extent the full and sustained force of an assimilationist policy.

The importance of community to art is illustrated by the words of the Hopi tribal chairman concerning the authenticity of katcina dolls as dependent upon participation in tribal ceremony (see chapter 2). As another artist put it, a tribal artist must follow the "cultural, artistic, and spiritual protocols" of the tribe (Thomas Jefferson Center 1993). Still another artist expressed the connection between community and art in a most thoughtful manner. He was, he said, raised in a world of art and artists and has been involved with many other tribes, but in no tribe that he has encountered is there a word in their language for "art"; rather, art is "incorporated into every aspect of our lives—it is in our religion, it is in our politics, it is in our social functions, it is in birth, it is in death. It is in that ever-encompassing circle we live within." He lamented, however, the fact that "we are now removing it from that context . . . and labeling it, and that can be detrimental to us if we begin to remove it and isolate it" (Atlatl 1992). Other expressions of the value of community focus on its role as a repository of tradition: "Our . . . strength is [that] we can practice our tradition today" (Atlatl 1992).

The most interesting perspectives—and most pertinent to the act—are those on the connections between tribal affiliation and identity as Indian. Some personal situations of nonenrolled artists were described in chapter 1. In chapter 5, the differences in attitude toward those who were not enrolled by the Dawes Commission were presented; they are relevant to the present-day attitude among some concerning affiliation. The individuals whose opinions are here expressed are not identified as being tribally enrolled or nonenrolled because (1) in not all cases is the enrollment status to be found in the data, and (2) those enrolled have a full range of opinions on the Indianness of nonenrolled individuals, as noted above. No one speaks on behalf of the pure wannabees, although there is disagreement among individuals about particular artists, as shown in chapter 4 regarding the alleged official Cheyenne pipemaker. Even Senator Campbell acknowledges that the law might prove to be unfair in practice and, if so, he is willing to see it amended (Sovereignty Symposium 1991).

One side of the argument favors the view of Indian identity as essentially sociocultural rather than as biologically based. This is expressed in the attitude that only the tribes can determine who is an Indian. The fierce adherence to this belief transcends the purely political right to determine members-as-citizens of a political entity. As I hope is apparent from the quoted statements, sovereignty, citizenship, community, tribal affiliation, and identity as Indian are all bound together. These themes inform the basic assumption that underlies the arguments of those who argue that tribal affiliation is requisite for Indian identity and identification. This assumption or belief is stated in a number of ways. It is not a matter of "blood quantum" but of "community recognition—if we as a community decide someone is Indian, we can include them" through the certification process (Atlatl 1992). "We know who we are" (Thomas Jefferson Center 1993). These attitudes affirm ethnicity theory, which requires ethnicity to have both subjective and objective attributes.

One very strong attitude was expressed by a number of participants: that an individual who claims to be Indian must seek out his or her tribe or community. There is certainly an undeniable logic to the view that only a tribe can be the ultimate authority as to who is an Indian. This logic is even stronger when specific tribal connections are involved. Can one claim to be a Navajo or Zuni or Cherokee if repudiated by the tribe? Senator Campbell takes the position that "if an artist is proud of advertising that he is a specific kind of Indian, then he should have no problem tracing his background, even if he is not enrolled." On the other hand, "If he cares so little about his heritage that he never has anything to do with the tribe from which he claims to have descended except to use it as a marketing ploy, or if the only way he can get his work sold is by advertising that he is Indian, then he should not be validated" (Viola 1993: 191).

This view, however, does not take into account the many ways in modern society that persons with Indian ancestry, with or without American Indian cultural attributes, have been separated from the tribal community. In that event, factors come into play concerning voluntary or involuntary alienation of Indian identity. In addition, some of the non-Indians under the act have not been separated from the tribe, such as the members of terminated tribes (the tribe as an ethnic community still exists and retains as a corporate entity any treaty rights it may have) and individuals who are a part of the tribal community but are not eligible for membership (like the Martinez children).

There is, of course, the other side of this argument, made by those who claim the law unfairly, perhaps unconstitutionally, excludes them from proclaiming the truth about their ancestry and heritage. This attitude is not limited to the nonenrolled individuals; it is also expressed by tribal people with relatives excluded or who foresee problems for their own descendants. For example, an enrolled Cherokee artist and museum director said that the act is "really a scary thing" because of the complexity of the Cherokee community, and she quoted from a press release which said that approximately one-third of the Master Artists in the Five Civilized Tribes Museum in Muskogee, Oklahoma, have a certification problem (Atlatl 1992). A photographer said she will remain faithful to the full-bloods who "hid in the mountains and the desert ravines and the Everglades and the redwoods and the canyons" to survive and to those who "refused to be a head count" (Atlatl 1992). She continued, "It has come to the point that we turn our backs. Has it come to a point that where [those with a] complex history, they do not fit into federal regulations, well, then they are invalid? And those who fall between the cracks, are they the price for authentic Indian art?"

A number of individuals expressed worry about a return to clannish or political tribal governments. Artist Jeanne R., whose situation was discussed by the Thomas Jefferson Center participants in Washington, D.C., noted that artists like herself are "at the mercy of 'government Indians.'" Because they are not enrolled members, they "have absolutely no vote or voice in our tribal leadership; yet we now have to ask that leadership for permission to express our personal heritage in our artwork" (U.S. Department of the Interior, 1991 files). The denial of certification by a tribe to nonenrolled artists will create conflict with a high probability of litigation.

II

Sovereignty and the reservation system are irrevocably interdependent, and the meaningful survival of American Indian culture depends on both. Wilkinson (1992: 23), a scholar of western law, likens the reservations to "a chain of islands within the greater society" and the system as the "heart of federal policy toward American Indians, . . . [a] system . . . in jeopardy." The "island" metaphor is apt:

> Indian societies—not every person within them, but the communities as whole cultures—are different. Their uniqueness is real and not based on romantic historical stereotypes. Life moves at a different pace. . . .
>
> The reservation system is essential to the preservation of Indian culture . . . Indians in the cities have sometimes made it as individuals but not as a culture . . . Indian culture has not survived in the cities because Indians are separatists. They are bound to their land and the sustenance, open space and protection it provides. Indians are island people. (94)

Wilkinson's "islands" are Deloria's "enclaves." An enclave is defined by *Webster's Third New International Dictionary* (1981) as a "territory enclosed within foreign territory." Deloria's writings emphasize the separatist viewpoint that, he says, reflects the Indian perspective rather than merely his personal views. The separatist perspective, according to Deloria, explains why American Indian activism differs from that of domestic American minorities (1974: 2–3). He argues, and makes a good case, that the domestic dependent nation status is similar to, and should be treated like, that of the small enclaves of Europe such as San Marino, Vatican City, and Liechtenstein (1985: 168–69).

Many of the individuals quoted in the foregoing pages are advocates of maintaining and expanding American Indian sovereignty and see the Indian Arts and Crafts Act as a positive step toward that goal. I suggest, however, that this is very dangerous territory. Pub. L. 101-644 blurs the lines of *tribal* prerogative by placing the state-recognized tribes, which do not have the government-to-government relationship with the federal government, on the same statutory footing as federally recognized tribes. The act also confuses the sovereign power to determine one's membership criteria by creating the category of certified artisans. Some legal conflict involving tribal governmental power over nonmembers is inevitable. Some tribes will end up being defendants in legal challenges by disgruntled nonmembers who are denied certification or who are certified but question any assumed authority of the tribe over them. Not only is complex litigation of this type very expensive to defend, but the real danger lies in the possibility that confusion of all these categories will weaken the claims of sovereignty. Certifying nonmember artisans is not, on its face at least, a *governmental* function—and tribal sovereignty is about *government*. The determination of criteria for member-citizens is an essential governmental exercise, perhaps the most basic. Fred L. Ragsdale analyzes the ramifications of the reaffirmed power of tribal governments and warns that, even as to legitimate governmental functions, many tribes may be moving too quickly. He cautions that "there should be a more careful analysis of the *interests at stake* before tribes try to expand their governmental powers to their theoretical limits" (1985: 79) (emphasis added). Federally recognized tribes should pick their sovereignty fights very carefully; from this admittedly distant view, the risk here seems greater than the prize to be won. Judicial opinions adverse to the certification authority could easily spill over onto the sovereign right to determine membership and undermine it. That possibility should be weighed against the advantages, if any, of certifying nonmember artisans.

III

According to James E. Falkowski, the entire scheme of Indian law throughout the Americas is racially based because it denies full political self-determination to indigenous peoples (1992). That position, obviously, has not been the one taken by the American courts.

In the United States, racial and ethnic classifications in law come within the reach of the Equal Protection Clause of the Fourteenth Amendment (for state action) and the Due Process Clause of the Fifth Amendment (for federal action). A classification based upon race or ethnic origin is not prohibited but is "suspect" and thus "subject to the most exacting scrutiny," which requires the government to prove that "the classification is necessary to a compelling interest" (Barron and Dienes 1991: 218). Indian law does appear to create such a classification by treating American Indians differently from non-Indian Americans. This treatment has been held to be constitutional because of the status of tribes as sovereign political entities: "Federal regulation of tribes . . . is governance of once-sovereign political communities; it is not to be viewed as legislation of a 'racial' group consisting of 'Indians' . . ." (Cohen 1982: 654, citing *United States v. Antelope*, 430 U.S. 641, 645–47 [1977]).

The treatment of federal Indian law as being nondiscriminatory because it is based on the status of Indian sovereignty rather than on race or national origin presumably does not, or should not, create a blanket exclusion for any law that somehow involves Indians. Thus, presumably, the Indian Arts and Crafts Act can be scrutinized by the federal courts to see if it creates a classification based on race or ethnic origin, and, if so, if it meets the constitutional test of being necessary to a compelling state interest. Is there anything about Pub. L. 101-644 that is racially based? The obvious question is whether forbidding the use of self-identification as Indian to those persons who are of Indian ancestry creates a racial classification and, if so, whether there is a compelling state interest in making such a classification. Another possibility is related to the comment made by Kimberly Craven, Congressman Campbell's aide (cited in the introduction) concerning the question of whether to include state-recognized tribes. Because they are not federally recognized, they do not have the special political government-to-government relationship with the federal government. Thus, if they are included simply because of their claim of descent from aboriginal peoples, they then constitute a racial rather than a political classification. Recognition by a state could be construed as creating political entities out of racial groups, but that would set a dangerous precedent.

The act's certification provision is not on the surface race-based, but if the 1993 opinion of the Solicitor-Indian Affairs (U.S. Department of the Interior 1993) is correct, and it probably is, then again the element of race (or ancestry) rather than political status is the basis. The general manager of the Indian Arts and Crafts Board, the agency charged with the task of formulating the regulations, requested the opinion. He asked how broadly the board could define "Indian product" to insure extending "federal protection to the greatest number of Indian individuals as possible for their creative work and associated economic benefits." The opinion logically defines "Indian product" as "an art or craft work produced by an Indian or Indian artisan." For the purposes of certification, however, the opinion states that "conceivably . . . an Indian tribe could certify anyone, irrespective of Indian blood, as an Indian artisan." It concludes that the intent of Congress was to limit certification to an individual of that tribe's lineage; thus "we think that a tribe may only certify persons of Indian blood as Indian artisans" (U.S. Department of the Interior 1993). The opinion is surely correct; that was most likely the intent. It does, however, put race back into this definition of Indian. As I discuss further below, there is a distinction between the *political* function of establishing criteria for membership/citizenship and the *non-political* function of certifying non-members as artisans. The latter could certainly be found racially discriminatory. I suggest that the authority to certify artisans, which is statutory, should not be equated with the sovereign authority to determine one's membership because conflict over the former could easily contaminate and undermine the latter.

IV

The confusion of the political with the cultural (or ethnic) and both with the racial seems to be endemic in all Indian matters in this country. The failure to make that distinction is arguably a major contributor to all contemporary conflict between Indians and non-Indians and, in the case of Pub. L. 101-644, between differently situated Indians as well. The political status as dependent-but-sovereign domestic nations distinguishes American Indians' legal status from that of all other ethnic groups in the United States. To some degree, the overlapping of the political and the cultural may be inevitable and the problems created thereby can only be minimized, not eliminated. I suggest that the Indian Arts and Crafts Act is an especially egregious example of this tendency. The failure to distinguish the two spheres is, I further suggest, the major flaw of the legislation as now written.

In their book entitled *The Road: Indian Tribes and Political Liberty* (1980), authors Barsh and Henderson offer a creative analysis of the legal and political status of American Indians in the United States today. They offer a "reconceptualization" that they hope will be "consistent with the experience of both tribal and nontribal citizens" to "provide *the road* for political reconciliation" (xiv–xv) (emphasis in original). They allude to the confusion of the political and the ethnic (or sociocultural), and the political and the racial at all levels in Indian and non-Indian society. They describe contemporary Indian movements as being focused on either the political or the ethnic. Although both are seen as adaptive strategies to federal policy, "they must be carefully separated in the public mind or both will fail. Indeed, they must also be separated in the minds of Indians" (243). And,

I might add, in the minds of lawyers, judges, and, especially, legislators.

Barsh and Henderson also cite the 1974 United States Supreme Court case of *Morton v. Mancari* (417 U.S. 535 [1974]) as a flagrant example of the confusion of political and racial categories. That case addressed the constitutionality of federal laws and regulations that gave hiring preference to members of federally recognized tribes for positions with the Bureau of Indian Affairs. The authors note that although Justice Blackmun stated that the preference was not racial but was established for the purpose of promoting tribal self-government through the Bureau of Indian Affairs, nevertheless he also opined that "if these laws . . . were deemed invidious racial discrimination, an entire Title of the United States Code (25 U.S.C.) would be effectively erased" (417 U.S. at 552, cited in Barsh and Henderson 1980: 242). The authors refer to Title 25, which is the codification of the large body of federal Indian law. They apparently read into the *Morton* opinion an uneasiness by the Supreme Court that the law may, in fact, be racially discriminatory, but that the court declined to decide that on the merits—that is, on the consideration of the facts, because it would upset a massive, well-entrenched scheme of long-standing precedence (242). They comment that "it should be kept in mind that the magnitude of an unconstitutional abuse of power is no justification of its continuance" (242). Noting that the "subfederal relationship" of the tribes to the federal government resides in hundreds of treaties, and considering congressional inconsistency in dealing with Indian affairs, they suggest the necessity of resolving them into "a single constitution of undisputed authority, presumably an amendment to our existing Constitution" (280).

V

Those who challenge the arts and crafts statute in court will attack it on various constitutional grounds, including the freedom of expression guarantee of the First Amendment, the Equal Protection Clause of the Fifth Amendment, and perhaps even the Privileges and Immunities Clause of Article IV, as suggested by one commentator (McSweeney 1993). These possible legal challenges are beyond the scope of this book, which is intended to address the social aspects inherent in the legislation itself. Nevertheless, discussion of some elements of possibly applicable law is appropriate to that end.

The First Amendment states that "Congress shall make no law abridging the freedom of speech." Freedom of expression was mentioned by both opponents and supporters of the act. Its supporters observe that there is no censorship issue since the act does not attempt to control content or sale; it only prohibits the marketing of work as Indian-made if it is not. The opponents counter that prohibitions on truthful marketing and promotion will deny to them their chosen form of livelihood.

The marketing aspect would constitute what is termed "commercial speech." Commercial speech is protected by the First Amendment, but less fully than noncommercial, especially political, speech, which itself is subject to some constraints. In *Virginia State Board of Pharmacy v. Virginia Citizens Consumer Council, Inc.* (425 U.S. 748, 96 S.Ct. 1817 [1976]), the United States Supreme Court determined that purely commercial speech, such as advertising, is protected subject to some governmental regulation. Among the constraints set by subsequent cases is the requirement that commercial speech be truthful. Wannabees aside, it is anyone's guess where the statements of a nonmember and noncertified artist who has Indian ancestry turn into untruthful commercial speech.

A related First Amendment problem is that of "chilled expression," which refers to the choice of an individual to forego testing the limits of free expression because of the possible legal sanctions he risks, not the least of which is financial. In the context of the Indian Arts and Crafts Act, that means that a seller of arts and crafts may fear asserting his or her Indianness, no matter how strongly he or she feels about it, because of the risk of imprisonment, fines, and/or civil penalties, even though the regulations provide that one can truthfully claim Indian descent.

VI

Congressional aide Kimberly Craven told the audience at the Oklahoma City public forum that the penalties for violation of the Indian Arts and Crafts Act of 1990 were intended to make it comparable to other intellectual property laws (Public Forum 1991). The trademark provisions, of course, deal with intellectual property, but redress would be found in the trademark statutes. I suggest that Pub. L. 101-644 can be read to create a new category of intellectual property—Indian identity. A number of participants in the various forums spoke of Indian identity in proprietary terms—as something that can be stolen from them and as a commodity. In chapter 4, several artists at the Atlatl forum were quoted as speaking of impostors who "ripped off" Indians and stole their identity as a "marketable commodity."

The statutory language lends some support to this possibility. It provides that the initiation of a civil action and the recovery of damages is available only to (1) an

Indian who is a member of an Indian tribe, (2) an Indian arts and crafts organization, or (3) a tribe on behalf of itself, a member, or an arts and crafts association—all as defined elsewhere in the statute. The consumer, who well may be the person most damaged monetarily, has no specific recourse under this act, although he or she does have normal channels of redress. The successful plaintiff under this act can recover not only punitive damages, but the "greater of" treble compensatory damages or, "in the case of *each* aggrieved individual Indian, Indian tribe, or Indian arts and crafts organization, *not less than* $1,000 for *each day* on which the offer or display for sale or sale continues" (25 U.S.C. 305[e][a]) (emphasis added). This $1,000 or more per day to each aggrieved party is neither compensatory nor punitive; perhaps it relates to the unauthorized appropriation of these parties' "property," their Indian identity.

If Indian identity is property, in which one has intellectual property rights, then the question arises whether those individuals who have a legitimate claim to being Indian by some accepted standard, but who are not Indians under this statute, have been deprived of their property without due process of law. The Fifth Amendment to the U.S. Constitution provides that "No person shall . . . be deprived of life, liberty, or property, without due process of law."

Let us assume for the sake of argument that Indian identity has been made intellectual property. Rosemary J. Coombe (1991) critiques the current state of intellectual property law in the context of critical legal theory and critical anthropology. She accepts the views of scholars in these fields concerning the negotiation of cultural and social reality as cultural constructs rather than as a dichotomy of objective and subjective realities. Traditional legal theory is based on "objectivist assumptions" that treat the world as "filled with determinate, mind-independent objects with inherent characteristics unrelated to human interaction" (1858, citing Steven Winter [1989]). The result is that "legal categories bear no accurate correspondence with a knowable reality" (1858). Intellectual property law has undergone "massive expansion of the cultural forms now considered to be private property" and the current state of the law is to expand "the ability to fix the signifier, because you 'own' the sign" (1866 n. 75, 1869).

> Those who attempt to give novel and alternative meanings to popular and powerful signifiers come up against the law and the politics of the commodity form. . . .
>
> If what is quintessentially human is the capacity to make meaning, challenge meaning, and transform meaning, then we strip ourselves of our humanity through over-zealous application and continuous expansion of intellectual property protections. Dialogue involves reciprocity in communication—the ability to respond to a sign with signs. What meaning does dialogue have when we are bombarded with . . . signs . . . whose significations cannot be challenged, and connotations we cannot contest? (1877, 1879)

What this implies is the possibility that if the Indian Arts and Crafts Act recognizes ownership of the sign ("Indian," "Native American") in "real" Indians (as defined by the act), then they can "fix" the signifier by determining who is an Indian through the sovereign right to determine membership and the statutory right to certify artisans. If the right to use Indian identity is a property right, can it be confined to the sale of arts and crafts? Will other ethnic groups be so empowered? Will other types of (nonethnic) identity follow? Farfetched? Probably.

The idea of protecting cultural rights is a concept that has expanded in recent years. "Cultural property" as a term dates from the 1954 Hague Convention, the UNESCO Convention for the Protection of Cultural Property in the Event of Armed Conflict, and it was further elaborated at the 1970 UNESCO Convention on the Means of Prohibiting and Preventing the Illicit Import, Export and Transfer of Ownership of Cultural Property (United Nations 1993: 50). That latter convention produced the following definition of cultural property: "property which, on religious or secular grounds, is specifically designated by each State as being of importance for archaeology, prehistory, history, literature, art or science." The concept of cultural property is not limited to tangible items; it also includes intellectual property, an area that the United States deals with generally in the legal context of patent, copyright, and trademark law. Cultural rights of American Indians took giant leaps forward (on paper, at least) with the enactments of the American Indian Religious Freedom Act in 1978 (AIRFA) (Pub. L. 95-341, 92 Stat. 469, codified in part 42 U.S.C. § 1996) and the Native American Graves Protection and Repatriation Act of 1990 (NAGPRA) (Pub. L. 101-601, 104 Stat. 3048). The latter mandates the return of certain human remains, burial goods, and religious objects; the former is noteworthy in providing for access to sacred sites.

If Indian/Native American/Aboriginal identity were to be considered intellectual property, it would most probably be analogous to that which is called "publicity rights" rather than to the more familiar areas of trademark, copyright, and patents. "Publicity rights" refers to the right of a celebrity, and sometimes his or her heirs, to control the use of the celebrity's image; the law has been developed primarily in the entertainment industry. It began in the 1940s and 1950s so that baseball celebrities could profit from the use of their photographic images on bubble-gum cards (Felcher and

Rubin 1980: 1125). That right itself seems to have been created by the courts through analogy, first to the right of privacy, then to rights in property, thus "publicity rights came to be a form of property rights." Felcher and Rubin note, however, that the problem with creating new areas of legal rights by analogy is that "they tend to impose a mature, elaborated system on what may well be an unformulated situation" (1127). This means, for example, that if Indian identity is analogized to publicity rights (or any other form of intellectual property), it will automatically become infused with the legal doctrine already built around those other distinctive areas. Property rights "are designed to grant individuals the power to exercise control over some entity, and to exclude others from exercising such control, largely for the purpose of creating economic incentives" (1128). Surely that sentence fits squarely the Indian Arts and Crafts Act if we replace "individuals" with "federally or state-recognized tribes and their members."

Felcher and Rubin suggest that the closest analogy of publicity rights is to copyright since both, unlike most property rights, often conflict with First Amendment rights. As we have seen, the right to foreclose another's use of Indian identity will conflict with that individual's right to freedom of expression, although at a yet undetermined point, or points.

David Lange suggests that "the growth of intellectual property in recent years has been uncontrolled to the point of recklessness" and that the "recognition of new intellectual property interests should be offset . . . by equally deliberate recognition of individual rights in the public domain" (1981: 147). He characterizes intellectual property as "having no existence of its own . . . apart from its recognition in law"; thus it has no discernible boundaries and is in that way different from most other forms of property (147). Because it is "subject to unlimited recreation in the mind of each observer . . . more than one person sensibly may assert a proprietary interest in what looks like the same property" (150). What could be the justification behind recognizing Indian identity as a property right? There is no evidence that Congress intended that result. Publicity rights are a relatively new form of intellectual property. Lange wonders why "suddenly the law should recognize claims in plaintiffs when recognition can come only at the expense of interests previously recognized in defendants" (164).

VII

The Indian Arts and Crafts Act does not directly address the content and style of artwork, although it may do so indirectly through provisions calling for the creation of "trademarks of genuineness and quality," whatever that may come to mean (25 U.S.C. 305[a][g][1]). Some regulations concerning standards and trademarks have been in existence since 1937 (25 CFR §§ 301–10 [1993]). They regulate the standards for Navajo, Pueblo, and Hopi silver and turquoise products, Navajo wool fabrics, Alaskan Indian and Eskimo handmade products, and the various trademarks and certificates to be used with them. As noted in the introduction, the regulations written by the Arts and Crafts board do define "Indian product" in terms of style, but thereby create a global category since they include items in both traditional and nontraditional styles and media. The regulations also define "handcrafts" in terms of limiting the devices that can be used in their production.

Content and style are certainly not the focus of the act, but at least one aspect of these features was deemed important by some of the forum participants. A number of them felt that fine arts should not be included within the scope of Pub. L. 101-644, that it should apply only to crafts. There is no clear distinction between those categories, of course, and they are capable of various interpretations. Nelson Graburn, for example, in discussing the indigenous art of the Fourth World, distinguishes between such categories as traditional or functional fine arts, commercial fine arts, souvenirs, reintegrated arts, assimilated fine arts, popular arts, and functional but noncommercial arts (1976: 5–10).

Senator Bingaman spoke to the U.S. Senate about his misgivings concerning the act and questioned the propriety of including both crafts and fine arts. He noted that European art forms, such as sculpture, oil painting, and watercolor painting, had been widely adopted by Indian artists, but that they did not need the same protection as traditional crafts, where the genuineness of the article is part of its inherent value.

> In addition to beauty, traditional Indian art represents a unique and irreplaceable way of life. Similar pieces made by non-Indians, or Indians of tribes for which the particular art has no inherent significance, would simply not be as valuable, no matter how skillful the imitation.
>
> In fine art, however, the same criteria do not apply. The value of the works are more exclusively in their aesthetic appeal, or value as investments, rather than in the cultural identity of the artist. For example, there is no identifiable style of Acoma oil painting, as there is with Acoma pottery. People cannot be readily deceived into believing that they are purchasing genuine Acoma oil paintings in the same manner that they can be deceived into thinking they are purchasing genuine Acoma pottery. (Bingaman 1991)

Senator Bingaman suggested that to attempt to regulate fine art "as we do traditional crafts . . . [has] merely injected

Congress into the debate over who has the right to call himself or herself an Indian, . . . a debate left, under the Constitution, to the Indian tribes as sovereign entities." The senator's distinction between fine arts and traditional crafts is one I believe better made, in the context of this statute, between "fake arts and crafts" and "fake Indians," who, nevertheless, produce genuine art. The senator and others who have expressed the need to make the distinction between fine arts and traditional crafts are only partially correct in their expression of the problem. Whereas a distinction can be made between fine arts and handcrafts in the context of the problem that produced the statute, the difference is exaggerated because of the completely different positions in the Indian arts and crafts industry of the two types of artists-craftspeople. The fine art is largely produced by Americans identifying themselves as Indians and the counterfeit crafts by foreign workers and entrepreneurs with no pretensions of being Indian producers, but whose products are sold as Indian-made. The statute has tackled two completely different problems with a single solution.

Should Congress decide to excise "fine arts" from the scope of Pub. L. 101-644, whose classification would, or should, be adopted? Despite the adoption of European-style media such as easel painting and the continuing evolution of traditional forms, nonetheless American Indian art must, and does, maintain its roots in its aboriginal forms of expression. An artist quoted earlier in this chapter noted the full integration of art into Indian life. Indian law scholar Rennard Strickland (1992: 182) characterizes this as the "holistic integration of life within art," which is an "underlying principle . . . held in common among Native Americans" (1992: 182). With regard to the difference between Western and Native American classification systems, he states that "the terms 'art,' 'artwork,' 'sacred,' and 'secular,' as non-Indians use them, embody concepts foreign to Native American societies. Among many Indian peoples, all human-made objects are grouped together and referred to as 'that which has been made.' The distinction between 'aesthetic objects,' 'sacred objects,' 'public objects,' and 'commercial objects' simply does not exist. In a holistic society, there are no such lines" (184). While we can assume that modern values have eroded somewhat that holistic purity, Strickland's observation does illustrate the hidden traps of ethnocentric classification in any ethnic-related law.

Graburn reminds us that Fourth World arts are always changing. He, too, addresses the development of nontraditional art forms in a way that illustrates the complex nature of the issues raised by the Indian Arts and Crafts Act (1976). J. J. Brody (1976: 82–83) discusses the development of easel painting in the Southwest from about the turn of the century. Whether it was an independent European-influenced development or one derived from traditional ceremonial painting, nevertheless:

> Except for a few years at San Ildefonso Pueblo, Indian easel painting was always a nontribal art with only the most tenuous roots in any tribal art system. Produced for urban-industrial consumers . . . it was assumed to be tribal, but as it developed in nontribal, antitribal, or pan-Indian environments, its forms could never be anything but nontribal, antitribal, or pan-Indian. If ever an art can be described as schizoid, it was Indian easel painting until it reached its most recent phase. In this phase, the problems cease to exist: It has no style, manner, tradition, nor anything else that identifies it as Indian; the artist simply happens to be Indian.

VIII

As discussed in chapter 3, Frances Svensson proposes that the tribes and the federal government need to determine where Indian identity is alienated. The Indian Arts and Crafts Act appears to create such a boundary marker, but fails. Considering the number of variables involved in any demarcation of Indianness in modern America and the inevitable differences of opinion, any attempt at a blanket marker is almost certainly doomed to arbitrariness. The statutory authority to certify artisans is perhaps recognition of this limitation and the need to make such a determination individual by individual (assuming there was an agreed-upon standard). But it also falls short in many ways. Still excluded, of course, are the many categories of persons mentioned throughout this book. But even those who have a tribe to which they can apply for membership or certification face possible inadequate criteria or arbitrary application processes.

A (painful) complication in the determination of alienation of identity arises from the involuntary nature of some types of alienation, most obviously in the many cases, prior to the enactment of the Indian Child Welfare Act of 1978 (25 U.S.C.A. §§ 1901-63), where Indian children were removed from the reservations and adopted into white families.

IX

Pub. L. 101-644 makes the definition of American Indians a dichotomous "is/is not" classification; an individual either is or is not an Indian. Judith D. Toland observes that "the concept that one cannot understand the meaning of what something is, unless the meaning of what something is not is articulated" is more basic than the holistic approach of multivariate analysis, but that "it is still the dynamic at work in the maintenance of cultural hegemony" in state-level political organization. She notes that there exist both subjective and objective aspects of ethnic identity—the subjective "who am I" and "who are we" have the objective corollary of the outsider's questions of "who is he, she, or they?" (1993: 7). This dichotomy is at work in the self-identification of an individual as an Indian and underlies the entire concept of the Indian Arts and Crafts Act.

It is unclear to what extent this dichotomy operated in the self-identification of artists with Indian ancestry prior to its formalization in the Indian Arts and Crafts Act. Most of the Indian art shows and art markets required one to be Indian, at least for the purpose of entering the shows, although proof and criteria varied. Some state statutes foreshadowed Pub. L. 101-644. In chapter 1, the comments of some artists on this new legal requirement to be Indian were cited. For example, John N. was quoted as saying that he never advertised his art as being Indian-made, but considered his art to be a reflection of his multifaceted heritage. A recent gallery brochure in my possession describes John N. as "born into a family of American Indian and Spanish descent." The act, therefore, imposes upon the Indian arts and crafts world a legally significant dichotomy of identification that did not necessarily preexist.

X

In the 1970s, anthropologists explored the concept of "imposed law," generally in the context of the colonial situation where the dominant society's alien legal system was viewed as imposed upon the subjugated peoples, which, according to Robert L. Kidder (1979: 289), was its "purest" form. Since then, scholars have realized that law is not just imposed upon subordinate peoples and groups by dominant groups, but is a dynamic and interactional system of "'codes,' discourses, and languages in which people pursue their varying and often antagonistic interests" (Starr and Collier 1989: 9). Imposed law was about political power: imposed law became passé, but power did not. Anthropologists write of "an emerging interest . . . in history and power relations in the study of law," of "a certain urgency to the kind of anthropology that is concerned with power," and how "capitalism organizes social inequality within groups by granting power to some and withholding it from others" (Starr and Collier 1989: 10; Nader 1988: 470; Collier 1993: 3).

It is difficult to think of laws emanating from Congress as being other than imposed, since most reflect not the "will of the people" but the influence of interest groups. But there are some interest groups that do not deserve the pejorative connotation applicable to those powerful lobbying groups with a public-be-damned attitude. Rather, these groups have a legitimate stake in promoting their interests. Pub. L. 101-644 began with the legitimate interests of those in the Indian arts and crafts industry, primarily in the Southwest, who were aggrieved by the flood of imported counterfeits. With the help of sympathetic congressmen—Senator Campbell is himself a jewelry-maker—their cause was taken up to Congress. During the legislative process, changes were made to accommodate the interests of two other categories of people—the nonenrolled artists and craftspeople of Native American ancestry and the state-recognized tribes. Thus, three sources of political power, each with a different interest, converged in the legislative process, and those interests reemerged in altered form. Perhaps political power, like energy, flows on and merely becomes transformed. The obvious power aspect resides in the creation of a very powerful federal law with the intended potential to deter or severely punish miscreants. This coercive power is direct. There is, however, a secondary power aspect—the creation by the statute of at least three power shifts. The most significant shift comes from the combination of the statutory definition of "Indian" and the certification provision. Now, nonenrolled artists who claim Indian ancestry must put themselves under the power of a federally or state-recognized tribe. That the exercise of that power may prove to be, in most cases, beneficent is beside the point. It is a shift in power, and within all power resides the potential for abuse. The other two power transformations may or may not have substance. Almost everyone involved believes that the statute creates a new avenue in which to exercise and expand the sovereign power of federally recognized tribes. I have argued above that such action would be counterproductive to the interests of those tribes. For the state-recognized tribes, the statute may prove to be an actual, if not formal, step toward federal recognition. That would, of course, decrease the power of the state over those groups and their members. Federal recognition disrupts many state powers, such as taxing authority, gaming regulation, and various other governmental functions.

XI

The Indian Arts and Crafts Act has not yet been interpreted by a court, and the final regulations have just been drafted to interject the administrative understanding of how the provisions should be carried out. This study has focused on the bare language of the statute and tried to provide some of the context embedding it. When litigation finally comes, the interpretation will depend upon the facts of the case presented and the court's reading of controlling law. Some of the principles guiding interpretation in certain areas of law are called "canons," which are rules of construction—in other words, how the statute is to be construed. In Indian law, the canons for treaty interpretation are intended to offset the disadvantageous position of the Native signatories. For example, treaties are to be interpreted "as they were understood by the tribal representatives who participated in their negotiation . . . [and] be liberally interpreted to accomplish their protective purposes, with ambiguities to be resolved in favor of the Indians" (Canby 1988:88) (citations omitted). These rules have been carried over to the interpretation of statutes—"statutes passed for the benefit of the dependent Indian tribes or communities are to be liberally construed, doubtful expressions being resolved in favor of the Indians"—as well as sometimes ignored (90; see also Cohen 1982: 221–25).

Cass R. Sunstein observes, in addition, that judicial interpretation depends upon what he calls "extratextual norms—understood as principles about constitutional government, institutional arrangements, basic fairness, and regulatory failure." He rejects the assertions of the "textualists" who believe that "the statutory language is the only legitimate basis for interpretation," that courts should not rely on outside sources (1990: 803). His argument is familiar to anthropologists:

> The textualist approach is inadequate. The central problem is that words are not self-defining; their meaning depends on both culture and context. There is no such thing as a pre-interpretive text, and words have no meaning before or without interpretation. To say this is not to say that words used in statutes can mean anything at all. . . . But it is to say that statutory terms are indeterminate standing "by themselves," and, more important, that they never stand by

> themselves. For this reason, background norms of interpretation, orienting the judicial reader to the text but not "in" it, are an indispensable part of interpretation. (804)

In addition to those background norms so widely shared as to be almost subconscious, there are nonshared and controversial norms, as well as linguistic problems such as "ambiguity, delegation or gaps, overinclusiveness, underinclusiveness, and changed circumstances" (805). The consequences of a strict textualist approach can be "irrationality, absurdity, or an inferior system of law" (807).

The "salutary corrective" is found in various kinds of background norms. The language of the statute or the administrative regulation constitutes "the instructions of the principal," which are "unintelligible without background norms that interpreters alone can supply" (Sunstein 808). The process of looking to the context of a statute or regulation results in the not uncommon, but always unsettling, case where a statute is held to mean exactly the opposite of what it appears to mean in ordinary language.

XII

The Indian Arts and Crafts Act is flawed structurally by its "apples and oranges" content. By that, I mean that it confuses or juxtaposes nonsimilar categories and treats them identically, with no recognition of the possible divergence of consequences. All of these poorly joined categories have been discussed separately in previous parts of this study. The first, and most significant, is the confusion of the political/legal, ethnic/cultural, social, and racial/biological usages for the term "Indian." Indian identity is based upon various combinations and degrees of these attributes. Another area where failure to make distinctions is important is that of tribal versus individual interests. United States law is not really set up to protect the interests of entities like the tribes, which is one reason why they have suffered such inconsistency in its application. As to individual rights, honed during the 1960s, one forum participant observed that many liberals "jump to support the individual" and forget about the rights and needs of the tribe or community (Thomas Jefferson Center 1993). Thus, when advocates for one position argue for the priority of tribal interests and those of the other for individual rights, they talk past one another. The interests of collectivity versus those of the individual is an inherent conflict in Indian law. This conflict was recognized in the creation of the Indian Bill of Rights (1968), which attempted to balance these competing interests by modifying, as restrictions on tribal governmental action, the Constitutional Bill of Rights, which protects the rights of American citizens, including Indians, against encroachment by state and federal governments.

A third distinction not made by the statute is between federally recognized and state-recognized tribes. There is a tremendous difference in the legal status of these two categories, as was discussed in chapters 2 and 3. States vary in the degree to which state recognition is meaningful at all, whereas federal recognition elevates a political entity to a category with a legal status of extraordinary magnitude—as a sovereign nation within the United States, with a government-to-government relationship with the federal government, which is largely beyond state control. Only one participant correctly addressed this issue. He stated that the rash of state recognitions in recent decades resulted from attempts to create tourist attractions and that such state actions are detrimental to federally recognized tribes that have a constitutional status. He called upon the federally recognized tribes to work to strike the provisions of the Indian Arts and Crafts Act that included the state-recognized tribes (Public Forum 1991).

Another distinction perceived by some and not accounted for is that between crafts and fine arts, discussed above. Still another distinction is that between what I have called "fake art" (the mostly imported counterfeit goods) and "fake Indians" (who may produce real art). I suggest that a satisfactory single solution to these very different problems is impossible.

The last distinction is between the interests of a federally recognized tribe in determining the criteria for their membership/citizenship, which is perhaps the most basic attribute of sovereignty, certainly one to be jealously guarded, and the authority, *statutory only*, to certify nonmember artisans. This blurring of the *sovereign right* to determine membership/citizenship with the *statutory authority* to certify nonmembers is, as I argued above, an opportunity for the former to be contaminated by the latter.

XIII

The title of this book is *The Arbitrary Indian: The Indian Arts and Crafts Act of 1990*. Arbitrariness reflects my initial impression upon learning of the act, and is, I believe, confirmed by my analysis. *Webster's Third New International Dictionary* (1981) defines "arbitrary" as based on "random or convenient selection or choice rather than on reason or nature" and as "arising from unrestrained exercise of the will, caprice, or personal preference." Pub. L. 101-644 is the result of these two types of arbitrariness—one of process and one of results.

On both federal and state levels, arbitrariness permeates the recognition process. The promulgation of administrative criteria and procedures for acknowledgement by the federal government and by some of the states represents a movement toward consistency and even-handedness. Nevertheless, the arbitrary element persists because Congress can, and does, legislate tribal recognition directly and because several of the states that recognize tribes have no criteria at all. At the congressional hearing on the Lumbee Recognition Act, a considerable number of tribes nationwide put into the record statements that opposed legislative recognition for any group and supported the application of a consistent set of criteria, such as that provided by the acknowledgement regulations (U.S. Congress, Senate 1991b). At another congressional hearing, the principal chief of the Eastern Band of Cherokee Indians spoke in strong support of "equitable criteria and an accepted process" for recognition of new tribes. He stated that "individual tribal recognition bills are unacceptable and can only lead to those groups with powerful or persistent Senators or Congressmen receiving recognition while those groups whose representatives are not as supportive will not achieve recognition regardless of the merits of either such group's claims. We further oppose such bills because the Congress itself has never adopted any criteria that are to be met" (U.S. Senate 1991a: 105). Additional processual arbitrariness crept in at the revision stage of the bill, when the certification provisions were drafted, apparently without much consideration for the implications, and when the state-recognized tribes were added, presumably as a result of pure politics and also without consideration of the implications.

The data and analysis offered in this study are also intended to demonstrate the arbitrary nature of the relationship between the purpose of the statute and its result. The class of people it defines as "Indian" is quite varied and includes (hypothetically) individuals with no or minimal indicia of

"Indianness" by descent and/or cultural traits. It potentially excludes full-bloods with a large complement of traditional sociocultural attributes. But such a class is arbitrary only in relation to the purpose of the statute. This is evident if we hypothesize a statute the purpose of which is to make these politically affiliated people eligible for some new benefit. In that event, the class called "Indian" is not arbitrary but perfectly fits the class of individuals singled out for the benefit.

I suggest, however, that Pub. L. 101-644 seeks to deter fraud by creating a class of persons with no logical connection to the desired results. This argument rests upon two assumptions and two assertations. The first assumption assumes the existence of individual artists or craftspeople excluded from the definition of "Indian" due to lack of membership in, or certification by, a federally or state-recognized tribe, but who would score high on any scale of Indianness based upon cultural, biological, and social criteria. This would include individuals such as full bloods who speak their native languages and are members of terminated tribes, or, like the children of Mrs. Martinez, who are ineligible for membership due to rules of patrilineality, matrilineality, or residence. The second assumption assumes the existence of artists or craftspeople who are included within the statutory language as "Indians" because they have the designated political affiliation despite minimal, if any, American Indian ancestry, social connections, or cultural attributes. This category might be represented by the members of a state-recognized tribe able to secure that status through political manipulation alone, without meeting meaningful criteria, or by an individual whose ancestor, Indian or not, appeared on the Dawes Rolls as a Cherokee and who came back to sign up despite a total lack of Indian-associated background. I do not include in this latter category individuals such as Yankton Sioux artist Chad N., because his adoption and acculturation do give him a valid claim to Indianness by standards that favor sociocultural over biological criteria. That the actual number of these anomalous individuals may be few is irrelevant both theoretically and practically—one properly situated plaintiff can fell a statute on constitutional grounds. In any event, there seems to be no data on the actual numbers and types of individuals potentially affected.

The first of my two assertions is that self-identification as Indian in the sale of art (or in any other circumstances) is an ethnic act (unless done by a wannabee, in which case it is fraud or self-delusion). This act of self-identification as an Indian may simultaneously be political, but it is still an ethnic act. The individuals legally permitted to perform this ethnic act are described not by the ethnic criteria, but by political criteria. Whereas those two could be identical, or at least very similar, in the United States today they are not. Furthermore, there are three very different types of political affiliations involved here: members of federally recognized tribes, members of state-recognized tribes, and artisans certified by either. These categories include extraordinary variations in criteria; indeed, in some cases, there are no criteria. Thus, I suggest that the lumping of these three categories into a class called "Indian" is virtually meaningless in terms of the problems the statute is intended to solve.

The second assertion is that self-identification in the sale of art is only one-half of a dialogue; the other party is the consumer, and the outcome a matter of negotiation. Thus, what the consumer (or consumers collectively) believe is or is not an Indian cannot be ignored. Some forum participants spoke with the realization that Indian arts and crafts, as an *industry*, depends upon the non-Indian public; others did not seem to share this belief. Howard Becker, in *Art Worlds* (1982), wrote of the institutionalized or organized sets of relationships among the many people involved in the production and sale of art, with the artist and the consumer at either end. Graburn, among others, uses the concept of the Fourth World to describe collectively "all aboriginal or native peoples whose lands fall within the national boundaries and techno-bureaucratic administrations of the countries of the First, Second, and Third Worlds" (1976: 1). Because these peoples are nonautonomous, their "very thought and culture reflect the differences from, and accommodation to, the realities of the majority peoples surrounding them." Therefore, "their arts are rarely produced for their own consumption or according to their own unmodified tastes." The study of these Fourth World Arts is "the study of *changing* arts—of emerging ethnicities, modifying identities, and commercial . . . stimuli" (2) (emphasis in original).

In 1969, Barth called for more study on ethnic boundaries, precipitating a good deal of research. Congress, however, has given new meaning to the concept of "boundaries" with Pub. L. 101-644. If we could map these boundaries, they would slash haphazardly across the contours of "Indianness" and take in only political affiliation, with a result that resembles nothing so much as that familiar political creature, the gerrymander. A more realistic boundary, if one is needed, would be that suggested by demographer Snipp, who distinguishes between the core population of easily identifiable "American Indians" with strong connections to their Indian backgrounds from those "Americans of Indian descent" who may have some Indian ancestry but have few or no Indian cultural attributes. This classification seems to echo that of the tribal members who support tribal membership as a criterion, but recognize that some legitimate Indians fall outside of that requirement.

The Indian Arts and Crafts Act of 1990 was not intended by Congress to be a major piece of Indian legislation, nor is it a significant expression of federal policy. It may adversely affect only a small number of individuals. That, however, is part of its significance for this analysis: *any* law, statutory or not, has the potential to change the entire legal structure of its context, rather like the camel's nose under the tent. Law and social change is not one-way, but interactional. Nor should benign intent obscure the issues. True intent is often hidden from public view in the legislative compromise negotiations. Beyond legislative intent, Kidder observes that "even if we could be confident of intent at the legislative level, we would still face endless corridors of cross-purposes at the level of legal administration and adjudication" (1979: 294).

One forum participant said that impostor Indians are a "problem in Indian life [which is] a larger issue than this act can address" (Thomas Jefferson Center 1993). I would expand that conclusion so that it applies to the entire issue of American Indian identity: it is a larger issue than this or any other single act can address and it raises the political question as to when, if at all, it is appropriate for the federal government to define American Indian identity and, in turn, how that should be done.

Appendix A

CIVIL STATUTE

25 U.S.C. § 305
(as amended by Pub. L. 101-644)

Short Title of 1990 Amendment

Pub. L. 101-644, title I, § 101, Nov. 29, 1990, 104 Stat. 4662, provided that: "This title [enacting sections 305d and 305e of this title, amending section 305a of this title and sections 1158 and 1159 of Title 18, Crimes and Criminal Procedure, and enacting provisions set out as a note under section 305e of this title] may be cited as the 'Indian Arts and Crafts Act of 1990'."

§ 305. Indian Arts and Crafts Board; creation and composition; per diem payments

A board is created in the Department of the Interior to be known as "Indian Arts and Crafts Board", and hereinafter referred to as the Board. The Board shall be composed of five commissioners, who shall be appointed by the Secretary of the Interior as soon as possible after August 27, 1935 and shall continue in office, two for a term of two years, one for a term of three years, and two for a term of four years from the date of their appointment, the term of each to be designated by the Secretary of the Interior, but their successors shall be appointed for a term of four years except that any person chosen to fill a vacancy shall be appointed for the unexpired term of the commissioner whom he succeeds. Both public officers and private citizens shall be eligible for membership on the Board. The Board shall elect one of the commissioners as chairman. One or two vacancies on the Board shall not impair the right of the remaining commissioners to exercise all the powers of the Board.

The commissioner shall serve without compensation: *Provided*, That each Commissioner shall be paid per diem in lieu of subsistence and other expenses at a rate that does not exceed the rate authorized by section 5703 of title 5 to be paid to persons serving without compensation.

(Aug. 27, 1935, ch. 748, § 1, 49 Stat. 891; Apr. 24, 1961, Pub. L. 87-23, 1, 75 Stat. 45.)

§ 305a.
Promotion of economic welfare through development of arts and crafts; powers of Board

It shall be the function and the duty of the Secretary of the Interior through the Board to promote the economic welfare of the Indian tribes and Indian individuals through the development of Indian arts and crafts and the expansion of the market for the products of Indian art and craftsmanship. In the execution of this function the Board shall have the following powers: (a) To undertake market research to determine the best opportunity for the sale of various products; (b) to engage in technical research and give technical advice and assistance; (c) to engage in experimentation directly or through selected agencies; (d) to correlate and encourage the activities of the various governmental and private agencies in the field; (e) to offer assistance in the management of operating groups for the furtherance of specific projects; (f) to make recommendations to appropriate agencies for loans in furtherance of the production and sale of Indian products; (g)(1) to create for the Board, or for an individual Indian or Indian tribe or Indian arts and crafts organization, trademarks of genuineness and quality for Indian products and the products of an individual Indian or particular Indian tribe or Indian arts and crafts organization; (2) to establish standards and regulations for the use of Government-owned trademarks by corporations, associations, or individuals, and to charge for such use under such licenses; (3) to register any such trademark owned by the Government in the United States Patent and Trademark Office without charge and assign it and the goodwill associated with it to an individual Indian or Indian tribe without charge; and (4) to pursue or defend in the courts any appeal or proceeding with respect to any final determination of that office; (h) to employ executive officers, including a general manager, and such other permanent and temporary personnel as may be found necessary, and prescribe the authorities, duties, responsibilities, and tenure and fix the compensation of such officers and other employees: *Provided*, That chapter 51 and subchapter III of chapter 53 of title 5 shall be applicable to all permanent employees and that all employees shall be appointed in accordance with the civil-service laws from lists of eligibles to be supplied by the Director of the Office of Personnel Management; (i) as a Government agency to negotiate and execute in its own name contracts with operating groups to supply management, personnel, and supervision at cost, and to negotiate and execute in its own name such other contracts and to carry on such other business as may be necessary for the accomplishment of the duties and purposes of the Board: *Provided*, That nothing in the foregoing enumeration of powers shall be construed to authorize the Board to borrow or lend money or to deal in Indian goods. For the purposes of this section, the term "Indian arts and crafts organization" means any legally established arts and crafts marketing organization composed of members of Indian tribes.

305b. Rules and regulations; submission to Secretary of the Interior

The Board shall prescribe from time to time rules and regulations governing the conduct of its business and containing such provisions as it may deem appropriate for the effective execution and administration of the powers conferred upon it by sections 305 to 305c of this title: *Provided*, That before prescribing any procedure for the disbursement of money the board shall advise and consult with the General Accounting Office: *Provided further,* That all rules and regulations proposed by the Board shall be submitted to the Secretary of the Interior and shall become effective upon his approval.

305c. Appropriation

There is authorized to be appropriated out of any sums in the Treasury not otherwise appropriated such sums as may be necessary to defray the expenses of the Board and carry out the purposes and provisions of sections 305 to 305c of this title. All income derived by the Board from any source shall be covered into the Treasury of the United States and shall constitute a special fund which is appropriated and made available until expended for carrying out the purposes and provisions of said sections. Out of the funds available to it at any time the Board may authorize such expenditures, consistent with the provisions of said sections, as it may determine to be necessary for the accomplishment of the purposes and objectives of said sections.

305d. Referral for criminal and civil violations; complaints; recommendations

(a) The Board may receive complaints of violations of section 1159 of title 18 and refer complaints of such violations to the Federal Bureau of Investigation for appropriate investigation. After reviewing the investigation report, the Board may recommend to the Attorney General of the United States that criminal proceedings be instituted under that section.

(b) The Board may recommend that the Secretary of the Interior refer the matter to the Attorney General for civil action under section 305e of this title.

305e. Cause of action for misrepresentation of Indian produced goods

(a) Injunctive or equitable relief; damages

A person specified in subsection (c) of this section may, in a civil action in a court of competent jurisdiction, bring an action against a person who offers or displays for sale or sells a good, with or without a Government trademark, in a manner that falsely suggests it is Indian produced, an Indian product, or the product of a particular Indian or Indian tribe or Indian arts and crafts organization, resident within the United States, to—

(1) obtain injunctive or other equitable relief; and

(2) recover the greater of—

(A) treble damages; or

(B) in the case of each aggrieved individual Indian, Indian tribe, or Indian arts and crafts organizations, not less than $1,000 for each day on which the offer or display for sale or sale continues.

(b) Punitive damages; attorney's fee

In addition to the relief specified in subsection (a) of this section, the court may award punitive damages and the costs of suit and a reasonable attorney's fee.

(c) Persons who may initiate civil actions

(1) A civil action under subsection (a) of this section may be commenced—

(A) by the Attorney General of the United States upon request of the Secretary of the Interior on behalf of an Indian who is a member of an Indian tribe or on behalf of an Indian tribe or Indian arts and crafts organization; or

(B) by an Indian tribe on behalf of itself, an Indian who is a member of the tribe, or on behalf of an Indian arts and crafts organization.

(2) Any amount recovered pursuant to this section shall be paid to the individual Indian, Indian tribe, or Indian arts and crafts organization, except that—

(A) in the case of paragraph (1)(A), the Attorney General may deduct from the amount recovered the amount for the costs of suit and reasonable attorney's fees awarded pursuant to subsection (b) of this section and deposit the amount of such costs and fees as a reimbursement credited to appropriations currently available to the Attorney General at the time of receipt of the amount recovered; and

(B) in the case of paragraph (1)(B), the amount recovered for the costs of suit and reasonable attorney's fees pursuant to subsection (b) of this section may be deducted from the total amount awarded under subsection (a)(2) of this section.

(d) Definitions

As used in this section—

(1) the term "Indian" means any individual who is a member of an Indian tribe; or for the purposes of this section is certified as an Indian artisan by an Indian tribe;

(2) the terms "Indian product" and "product of a particular Indian tribe or Indian arts and crafts organization" has the meaning given such term[1] in regulations which may be promulgated by the secretary of the Interior;

(3) the term "Indian tribe" means—

(A) any Indian tribe, band, nation, Alaska Native village, or other organized group or community which is recognized as eligible for the special programs and services provided by the United States to Indians because of their status as Indians; or

(B) any Indian group that has been formally recognized as an Indian tribe by a State legislature or by a State commission or similar organization legislatively vested with State tribal recognition authority; and

(4) the term "Indian arts and crafts organization" means any legally established arts and crafts marketing organization composed of members of Indian tribes.

(e) Severability

In the event that any provision of this section is held invalid, it is the intent of Congress that the remaining provisions of this section shall continue in full force and effect.

[1]So in original. Probably should be "terms".

Appendix B

CRIMINAL STATUTE

18 U.S.C. §§ 1158 and 1159 (as amended by Pub. L. 101-644)

§ 1158. Counterfeiting Indian Arts and Crafts Board trade mark

Whoever counterfeits or colorably imitates any Government trade mark used or devised by the Indian Arts and Crafts Board in the Department of the Interior as provided in section 305a of Title 25, or, except as authorized by the Board, affixes any such Government trade mark, or knowingly, willfully, and corruptly affixes any reproduction, counterfeit, copy, or colorable imitation thereof upon any products, or to any labels, signs, prints, packages, wrappers, or receptacles intended to be used upon or in connection with the sale of such products; or

Whoever knowingly makes any false statement for the purpose of obtaining the use of any such Government trade mark—

Shall (1) in the case of a first violation, if an individual, be fined not more than $250,000 or imprisoned not more than five years, or both, and, if a person other than an individual, be fined not more than $1,000,000; and (2) in the case of subsequent violations, if an individual, be fined not more than $1,000,000 or imprisoned not more than fifteen years, or both, and, if a person other than an individual, be fined not more than $5,000,000; and (3) shall be enjoined from further carrying on the act or acts complained of.

(As amended Nov. 29, 1990, Pub. L. 101-644, title I. § 106, 104 Stat. 4665.)

(a) It is unlawful to offer or display for sale or sell any good, with or without a Government trademark, in a manner that falsely suggests it is Indian produced, and Indian product, or the product of a particular Indian or Indian tribe or Indian arts and crafts organization, resident within the United States.

(b) Whoever knowingly violates subsection (a) shall—

(1) in the case of a first violation, if an individual, be fined not more than $250,000 or imprisoned not more than five years, or both, and, if a person other than an individual, be fined not more than $1,000,000; and

(2) in the case of subsequent violations, if an individual, be fined not more than $1,000,000 or imprisoned not more than fifteen years, or both, and, if a person other than an individual, be fined not more than $5,000,000.

(c) As used in this section—

(1) the term "Indian" means any individual who is a member of an Indian tribe, or for the purposes of this section is certified as an Indian artisan by an Indian tribe;

(2) the terms "Indian product" and "product of a particular Indian tribe or Indian arts and crafts organization" has the meaning given such term in regulations which may be promulgated by the Secretary of the Interior;

(3) the term "Indian tribe" means—

(A) any Indian tribe, band, nation, Alaska Native village, or other organized group or community which is recognized as eligible for the special programs and services provided by the United States to Indians because of their status as Indians; or

(B) any Indian group that has been formally recognized as an Indian tribe by a State legislature or by a State commission or similar organization legislatively vested with State tribal recognition authority; and

(4) the term "Indian arts and crafts organization" means any legally established arts and crafts marketing organization composed of members of Indian tribes.

(d) In the event that any provision of this section is held invalid, it is the intent of Congress that the remaining provisions of this section shall continue in full force and effect.

(As amended Nov. 29, 1990, Pub. L. 101-644, title I, § 104(a), 104 Stat. 4663.)

Appendix C

FEDERAL ACKNOWLEDGMENT PROCEDURE

25 C.F.R. § 83 (1993)

Part 83—Procedures for establishing That an American Indian Group Exists as an Indian Tribe

Sec.

AUTHORITY: 5 U.S.C. 301; secs. 463 and 465 of the Revised Statutes, 25 U.S.C. 2 and 9; and 230 DM 1 and 2.

SOURCE: 43 FR. 39361, Sept. 5, 1978, unless otherwise noted. Redesignated at 47 FR 13327, Mar. 30, 1982.

§ 83.1 Definitions

(a) *Secretary* means the Secretary of the Interior or his authorized representative.

(b) *Assistant Secretary* means the Assistant Secretary—Indian Affairs, or his authorized representative

(c) *Department* means the Department of the Interior.

(d) *Bureau* means the Bureau of Indian Affairs.

(e) *Area Office* means the Bureau of Indian Affairs Area Office.

(f) *Indian tribe,* also referred to herein as *tribe,* means any Indian group within the continental United States that the

Secretary of Interior acknowledges to be an Indian tribe.

(g) *Indian group or group* means any Indian aggregation within the continental United States that the Secretary of the Interior does not acknowledge to be an Indian tribe.

(h) *Petitioner* means any entity which has submitted a petition to the Secretary requesting acknowledgment that it is an Indian tribe.

(i) *Autonomous* means having a separate tribal council, internal process, or other organization mechanism which the tribe has used as its own means of making tribal decisions independent of the control of any other Indian governing entity. Autonomous must be understood in the context of the Indian culture and social organization of that tribe.

(j) *Member of an Indian group* means an individual who is recognized by an Indian group as meeting its membership criteria and who consents to being listed as a member of that group.

(k) *Member of an Indian tribe* means an individual who meets the membership requirements of the tribe as set forth in its governing document or is recognized collectively by those persons comprising the tribal governing body, and has continuously maintained tribal relations with the tribe or is listed on the tribal rolls of that tribe as a member, if such rolls are kept.

(l) *Historically, historical* or *history* means dating back to the earliest documented contact between the aboriginal tribe from which the petitioners descended and citizens or officials of the United States, colonial or territorial governments, or if relevant, citizens and officials of foreign governments from which the United States acquired territory.

(m) *Continuously* means extending from generation to generation throughout the tribe's history essentially without interruption.

(n) Indigenous means native to the continental United States in that at least part of the tribe's aboriginal range extended into what is now the continental United States.

(o) *Community* or *specific area* means any people living within such a reasonable proximity as to allow group interaction and maintenance of tribal relations.

(p) *Other party* means any person or organization, other than the petitioner who submits comments or evidence in support of or in opposition to a petition.

§ 83.2 Purpose

The purpose of this part is to establish a departmental procedure and policy for acknowledging that certain American Indian tribes exist. Such acknowledgment of tribal existence by the Department is a prerequisite to the protection, services, and benefits from the Federal Government available to Indian tribes. Such acknowledgment shall also mean that the tribe is entitled to the immunities and privileges available to other federally acknowledged Indian tribes by virtue of their status as Indian tribes as well as the responsibilities and obligations of such tribes. Acknowledgment shall subject the Indian tribe to the same authority of Congress and the United State to which other federally acknowledged tribes are subjected.

§ 83.3 Scope

(a) This part is intended to cover only those American Indian groups indigenous to the continental United States which are ethnically and culturally identifiable, but which are not currently acknowledged as Indian tribes by the Department. It is intended to apply to groups which can establish a substantially continuous tribal existence and which have functioned as autonomous entities throughout history until the present.

(b) This part does not apply to Indian tribes, organized bands, pueblos or communities which are already acknowledged as such and are receiving services from the Bureau of Indian Affairs.

(c) This part is not intended to apply to associations, organizations, corporations or groups of any character, formed in recent times; provided that a group which meets the criteria in § 87.7 (a) through (g) has recently incorporated or otherwise formalized its existing autonomous process will have no bearing on the Assistant Secretary's final decision.

(d) Nor is this part intended to apply to splinter groups, political factions, communities or groups of any character which separate from the main body of a tribe currently acknowledged as being an Indian tribe by the Department, unless it can be clearly established that the group has functioned throughout history until the present as an autonomous Indian tribal entity.

(e) Further, this part does not apply to groups which are, or the members of which are, subject to congressional legislation terminating or forbidding the Federal relationship.

§ 83.4 Who may file.

Any Indian group in the continental United States which believes it should be acknowledged as an Indian tribe, and can satisfy the criteria in § 83.7, may submit a petition requesting that the Secretary acknowledge the group's existence as an Indian tribe.

§ 83.5 Where to file.

A petition requesting the acknowledgment that an Indian group exists as an Indian tribe shall be filed with the Assistant Secretary—Indian Affairs, Department of the Interior, 18th and "C" Streets NW., Washington, DC 20245. Attention: Federal acknowledgment project.

§ 83.6
Duties of the Department

(a) The Department shall assume the responsibility to contact, within a twelve-month period following the enactment of these regulations, all Indian groups known to the Department in the continental United States whose existence has not been previously acknowledged by the Department. Included specifically shall be those listed in chapter 11 of the American Indian Policy Review commission final report, volume one, May 17, 1977. The Department shall inform all such groups of the opportunity to petition for an acknowledgment of tribal existence by the Federal Government.

(b) The Secretary shall publish in the FEDERAL REGISTER

within 90 days after effective date of these regulations, a list of all Indian tribes which are recognized and receiving services from the bureau of Indian Affairs. Such list shall be updated and published annually in the FEDERAL REGISTER.

(c) Within 90 days after the effective date of the final regulations, the Secretary will have available suggested guidelines for the format of petitions, including general suggestions and guidelines on where and how to research for required information. The Department's example of petition format, while preferable, shall not prelude the use of any other format.

(d) The Department shall, upon request, provide suggestions and advice to researchers representing a petitioner for their research into the petitioner's historical background and Indian identity. The Department shall not be responsible for the actual research on behalf of the petitioner.

§ 83.7 Form and content of the petition

The petition may be in any readable form which clearly indicates that it is a petition requesting the Secretary to acknowledge tribal existence. All the criteria in paragraphs (a) through (g) of this section are mandatory in order for tribal existence to be acknowledged and must be included in the petition.

(a) A statement of facts establishing that the petitioner has been identified from historical times until the present on a substantially continuous basis, as "American Indian," or "aboriginal." A petitioner shall not fail to satisfy any criteria herein merely because of fluctuations of tribal activity during various years. Evidence to be relied upon in determining the group's substantially continuous Indian identity shall include one or more of the following:

(1) Repeated identification by Federal authorities;

(2) Longstanding relationships with State governments based on identification of the group as Indian;

(3) Repeated dealings with a county, parish, or other local government in a relationship based on the group's Indian identity;

(4) Identification as an Indian entity by records in courthouses, churches, or schools;

(5) Identification as an Indian entity by anthropologists, historians, or other scholars;

(6) Repeated identification as an Indian entity in newspapers and books;

(7) Repeated identification and dealings as an Indian entity with recognized Indian tribes or national Indian organizations.

(b) Evidence that a substantial portion of the petitioning group inhabits a specific area or lives in a community viewed as American Indian and distinct from other populations in the area, and that its members are descendants of an Indian tribe which historically inhabited a specific area.

(c) A statement of facts which establishes that the petitioner has maintained tribal political influence or other authority over its members as an autonomous entity throughout history until the present.

(d) A copy of the group's present governing document, or in the absence of a written document, a statement describing in full the membership criteria and the procedures through which the group currently governs its affairs and its members.

(e) A list of all known current members of the group and a copy of each available former list of members based on the tribe's own defined criteria. The membership must consist of individuals who have established, using evidence acceptable to the Secretary, descendancy from a tribe which existed historically or from historical tribes which combined and functioned as a single autonomous entity. Evidence acceptable to the Secretary of tribal membership for this purpose includes but is not limited to:

(1) Descendancy rolls prepared by the Secretary for the petitioner for purposes of distributing claims money, providing allotments, and other purposes;

(2) State, Federal, or other official records or evidence identifying present members of ancestors of present members as being an Indian de-

scendant and a member of the petitioning group;

(3) Church, school, and other similar enrollment records indicating the person as being a member of the petitioning entity;

(4) Affidavits of recognition by tribal elders, leaders. or the tribal governing body, as being an Indian descendant of the tribe and a member of the petitioning entity;

(5) Other records or evidence identifying the person as a member of the petitioning entity.

(f) The membership of the petitioning group is composed principally of persons who are not members of any other North American Indian tribe.

(g) The petitioner is not, nor are its members, the subject of congressional legislation which has expressly terminated or forbidden the Federal relationship.

§ 83.8 Notice of receipt of petition.

(a) Within 30 days after receiving a petition, the Assistant Secretary shall send an acknowledgment of receipt, in writing, to the petitioner, and shall have published in the FEDERAL REGISTER a notice of such receipt including the name and location, and mailing address of the petitioner and other such information that will identify the entity submitting the petition and the date it was received. The notice shall also indicate where a copy of the petition may be examined.

(b) Groups with petitions on file with the Bureau on the effective date of these regulations shall be notified within 90 days from the effective date that their petition is on file. Notice of that fact, including the information required in paragraph (a) of this section, shall be published in the FEDERAL REGISTER. All petitions on file on the effective date will be returned to the petitioner with guidelines as specified in § 83.6(c) in order to give the petitioner an opportunity to review, revise, or supplement the petition. The return of the petition will not affect the priority established by the initial filing.

(c) The Assistant Secretary shall also notify, in writing, the Governor and attorney general of any State in which a petitioner resides.

(d) The Assistant Secretary shall also cause to be published the notice of receipt of the petition in a major newspaper of general circulation in the town or city nearest to the petitioner. The notice will include, in addition to the information in paragraph (a) of this section, notice of opportunities for other parties to submit factual or legal arguments in support of or in opposition to the petition. Such submissions shall be provided to the petitioner upon receipt by the Federal acknowledgement staff. The petitioner shall be provided an opportunity to respond to such submissions prior to a final determination regarding the petitioner's status.

§ 83.9 Processing the petition

(a) Upon receipt of a petition, the Assistant Secretary shall cause a review to be conducted to determine whether the petitioner is entitled to be acknowledged as an Indian tribe. The review shall include consideration of the petition and supporting evidence, and the factual statements contained therein. The Assistant Secretary may also initiate other research by his staff, for any purpose relative to analyzing the petition and obtaining additional information about the petitioner's status, and may consider any evidence which may be submitted by other parties.

(b) Prior to actual consideration of the petition, the Assistant Secretary shall notify the petitioner of any obvious deficiencies, or significant omissions, that are apparent upon an initial review, and provide the petitioner with an opportunity to withdraw the petition for further work or to submit additional information or a clarification.

(c) Petitions shall be considered on a first come, first serve basis determined by the date of original filing with the Department. The Federal acknowledgment project staff shall establish a priority register including those petitions already pending before the Department.

(d) The petitioner and other parties submitting comments on the petition shall be notified when the petition comes under active consideration. They shall also be notified who is the primary Bureau staff member reviewing the petition, his backup, and supervisor. Such notices shall also include the office address and telephone number of the primary staff member.

(e) A petitioning group may, at its option and upon written request, withdraw its petition prior to publication by the Assistant Secretary of his finding in the FEDERAL REGISTER and, may if it so desires, file an entirely new petition. Such petitioners shall not lose their priority date by withdrawing and resubmitting their petitions later, provided the time periods in paragraph (f) of this section shall begin upon active consideration of the resubmitted petition.

(f) Within 1 year after notifying the petitioner that active consideration of the petition has begun, the Assistant Secretary shall publish his proposed findings in the FEDERAL REGISTER. The Assistant Secretary may extend that period up to an additional 180 days upon a showing of due cause to the petitioner. In addition to the proposed findings, the Assistant Secretary shall prepare a report which shall summarize the evidence for the proposed decision. Copies of such report shall be available for the petitioner and other parties upon written request.

(g) Upon publication of the proposed findings, any individual or organization wishing to challenge the proposed findings shall have a 120-day response period to present factual or legal arguments and evidence to rebut the evidence relied upon.

(h) After consideration of the written arguments and evidence rebutting the proposed findings, the Assistant Secretary shall make a determination regarding the petitioner's status, a summary of which shall be published in the FEDERAL REGISTER within 60 days from the expiration of the response period. The determination will become effective in 60 days from publication unless earlier withdrawn pursuant to § 83.10.

(i) The Assistant Secretary shall acknowledge the existence of the petitioner as an Indian tribe when it is determined that the group satisfied the criteria in § 83.7.

(j) The Assistant Secretary shall refuse to acknowledge that a petitioner is an Indian tribe if it fails to satisfy the criteria in § 83.7. In the event the Assistant Secretary refuses to acknowledge the eligibility of a petitioning group, he shall analyze and forward to the petitioner other options, if any, under which application for services and other benefits may be made.

§ 83.10 Reconsideration and final action.

(a) The Assistant Secretary's decision shall be final for the Department unless the Secretary requests him to reconsider within 60 days of such publication. If the Secretary recommends reconsideration, the Assistant Secretary shall consult with the Secretary, review his initial determination, and issue a reconsidered decision within 60 days which shall be final and effective upon publication.

(b) The Secretary in his consideration of the Assistant Secretary's decision may review any information available to him whether formally part of the record or not; where reliance is placed on information not of record, such information shall be identified as to source and nature, and inserted in the record.

(c) The Secretary may request reconsideration of any decision by the Assistant Secretary but shall request reconsideration of any decision, which in his opinion:

(1) Would be changed by significant new evidence which he has received subsequent to the publication of the decision; or

(2) A substantial portion of the evidence relied on was unreliable or was of little probative value; or

(3) The petitioner's or the Bureau's research appears inadequate or incomplete in some material respect.

(d) Any notice which by the terms of these regulations must be published in the FEDERAL REGISTER, shall also be mailed to the petitioner, the Governors and attorney generals of the States involved, and to other parties which have commented on the proposed findings.

§ 83.11
Implementation of decisions

(a) Upon final determination that the petitioner is an Indian tribe, the tribe shall be eligible for services and benefits from the Federal Government available to other federally recognized tribes and entitled to the privileges and immunities available to other federally recognized tribes by virtue of their status as Indian tribes with a government-to-government relationship to the United States as well as having the responsibilities and obligations of such tribes. Acknowledgment shall subject such Indian tribes to the same authority of Congress and the United States to which other federally acknowledged tribes are subject.

(b) While the newly recognized tribe shall be eligible for benefits and services, acknowledgment of tribal existence will not create an immediate entitlement to existing Bureau of Indian Affairs programs. Such programs shall become available upon appropriation of funds by Congress. Requests for appropriations shall follow a determination of the needs of the newly recognized tribe.

(c) Within 6 months after acknowledgment that the petitioner exists as an Indian tribe, the appropriate Area Office shall consult and develop in cooperation with the group, and forward to the Assistant Secretary, a determination of needs and a recommended budget required to serve the newly acknowledged tribe. The recommended budget will be considered along with other recommendations by the Assistant Secretary in the usual budget-request process.

Appendix D

FINAL REGULATIONS TO IMPLEMENT THE INDIAN ARTS AND CRAFTS ACT OF 1990

On October 21, 1996, the *Federal Register* published the final regulations for the Indian Arts and Crafts Act of 1990, Public Law 101-644, with a number of typographical errors. This version of the final regulations contains the original and correct text.

DEPARTMENT OF THE INTERIOR

Indian Arts and Crafts Board

25 CFR Part 309
RIN 1090-AA45
Protection for Products of Indian Art and Craftsmanship

AGENCY: Indian Arts and Crafts Board (IACB), DOI

ACTION: Final Rule.

SUMMARY: This rule adopts regulations to carry out Public Law 101-644, the Indian Arts and Crafts Act of 1990. The regulations define the nature and Indian origin of products that the law covers and specify procedures for carrying out the law. The trademark provisions of the Act are not included in this rulemaking and will be treated at a later time.

EFFECTIVE DATES: November 20, 1996.

FOR FURTHER INFORMATION CONTACT: Meridith Z. Stanton or Geoffrey E. Stamm, Indian Arts and Crafts Board, Room 4004-MIB, U. S. Department of the Interior, 1849 C Street, NW., Washington, DC 20240, telephone 202-208-3773 (not a toll-free call).

SUPPLEMENTARY INFORMATION:

Background

The Act of August 27, 1935 (49 Stat. 891; 25 U.S.C. 305 et seq.; 18 U.S.C. 1158–59), created the Indian Arts and Crafts Board. The Board is responsible for promoting the development of American Indian and Alaska Native arts and crafts, improving the economic status of members of Federally-recognized tribes, and helping to develop and expand marketing opportunities for arts and crafts produced by American Indians and Alaska Natives.

The 1935 Act adopted criminal penalties for selling goods with misrepresentations that they were Indian produced. This provision, currently located in section 1159 of title 18, United States Code, set fines not to exceed $500 or imprisonment not to exceed six months, or both. Although this law was in effect for many years, it provided no meaningful deterrent to those who misrepresent imitation arts and crafts as Indian produced. In addition, it required "willful" intent to prove a violation, and very little enforcement took place.

In response to growing sales in the billion dollar U.S. Indian arts and crafts market of products misrepresented or erroneously represented as produced by Indians, the Congress passed the Indian Arts and Crafts Act of 1990. This Act is essentially a truth-in-advertising law designed to prevent marketing products as "Indian made" when the products are not, in fact, made by Indians as defined by the Act.

Public Participation

The Indian Arts and Crafts Board published the proposed rulemaking for the Indian Arts and Crafts Act of 1990 on October 13, 1994. 59 FR 51908–51911. As the Federal Register omitted several key lines from the Enforcement section 309.3, the Federal Register published a correction on October 18, 1994. 59 FR 52588.

In addition to publication, several thousand copies of the proposed rulemaking were distributed to interested parties, including every Federally-recognized Indian tribe.

The Board received 36 public comments on the proposed rulemaking, and each was carefully reviewed, analyzed, and considered. These comments are grouped by issues and Board responses in the following summary.

Summary and Analysis of Public Comments

A broad range of respondents expressed their support of the proposed regulations. These comments emphasized the crucial contribution of art and craft work production and sales to the economic development of Indian individuals and tribes throughout the nation.

Overall Comments

Several comments raised the issue of what is a reasonable boundary between marketing statements that are simply truthful and statements that are clearly misleading. One respondent expressed concern that the Act and proposed regulations prohibit an artist who is not a member of an Indian tribe from truthfully describing his or her Indian heritage as part of the discussion of his or her art work. The regulations do not prohibit any statements about a person's Indian heritage that are truthful and not misleading in the marketing of that individual's work.

One comment asked whether an individual, who is neither enrolled nor certified as an Indian artisan, is permitted under the Act to use the term "Non-Government Enrolled Descendant" or its abbreviation, "NGED," in conjunction with the name of an Indian tribe to market his or her work. Considered as a whole, this phrase and its abbreviation are misleading. The capitalization implies some sort of official standing, and the word "enrolled" is positive. However, the truth is exactly the opposite: the individual is not officially recognized by, and is not enrolled in, the tribe named.

One comment questioned the treatment of persons of various degrees of Indian ancestry who are active in the art market, but are not members of tribes. As described in section 309.3

of the Section-by-Section Comments, Congress in the Act addressed this situation by leaving it to the tribes to decide whether to certify as Indian artisans for purposes of the Act individuals who have some degree of ancestry of that tribe but are not tribal members. This tribal certification method also is discussed in section 309.4 of the regulations. A person is permitted under the regulations to make a truthful statement, in connection with marketing of an art or craft product, that he or she is of Indian "descent" or particular tribal "descent."

Several respondents questioned the absence of regulations implementing the Act's trademark provisions and recommended that a supplementary rule be proposed for comment, to carry out the trademark section, before final publication of the regulations. This recommendation has not been adopted. The Indian Arts and Crafts Board is not prepared to carry out the trademark section of the Act at this time. Although the trademark provisions may be desirable in their own right, they are not necessary to the protections covered by these regulations. As stated previously, the trademark provisions of the Act will be treated at a later time.

One comment recommended and advocated changes in both the proposed regulations and the Act on the grounds that they are unconstitutional. Another comment asked for a repeal of the Act and proposed regulations, as they are a violation of the freedom of speech of all "Indian Americans." These comments have not been adopted either. While regulations can interpret and clarify the Act, regulations cannot change the Act. Furthermore, the regulations do not prohibit any individual, marketing enterprise, or other vendor from truthfully representing the art or craft products that they offer or display for sale or sell. The regulations define the nature and Indian origin of products protected by the Indian Arts and Crafts Act of 1990, a truth-in marketing law, from false representations. They also specify how the Indian Arts and Crafts Board will interpret certain conduct for enforcement purposes.

Finally, several comments recommended that the regulations be reissued in proposed form for further comment before final publication of the regulations to carry out the Act. A broad range of comments was received and carefully considered. Appropriate revisions and refinements have been adopted without fundamental change to the approach of the proposed regulations. Accordingly reissuance in proposed form is not warranted.

Section-by-Section Comments

Section 309.1 How Do the Regulations in This Part Carry out the Indian Arts and Crafts Act of 1990?

One response asked how the legislation affects arts and crafts sold in business establishments. Another stated that the "middle man" should be held accountable for how the product is marketed.

Section 309.1 of the regulations covers these concerns. It states that the Act regulates products offered or displayed for sale, or sold as Indian produced, an Indian product, or the product of a particular Indian, or Indian tribe, or Indian arts and crafts organization within the United States. This section does not limit the marketing vehicles covered by the regulations. The Act applies to any offer for sale or display for sale, or actual sale by any person in the United States. In light of this broad application, section 309.1 is appropriately drafted.

Section 309.2 What Are the Key Definitions for Purposes of the Act?

Definition of Indian, Section 309.2(a)

One respondent asked that the regulations specifically name Native Hawaiians to protect them under the Act. Another wanted individuals who have Certificates of Indian Blood, yet are neither on tribal rolls nor certified as Indian artisans, to be included under the definition of Indian.

The final regulations do not adopt these suggestions. The

Act specifically defines who is an Indian protected by the Act. The regulations can interpret and clarify the Act but cannot change the statutory terms of the Act.

One respondent expressed concern about state incorporated non-profit "Indian" organizations and their members who are not enrolled with state or Federally-recognized tribes, yet present themselves as Indian at crafts shows. In addition, adoption was an issue for two respondents. One expressed concern that non-Indians, "adopted by Indian spiritual leaders," may be permitted to sell their work as Indian. Another stated that "not until the seventh generation" should an adopted tribal member or family have the right to offer their handcrafts for sale as Indian.

The definition of Indian already satisfies these concerns. State incorporated non-profit "Indian" organizations do not meet the definition of Indian tribe under the Act and in section 309.2(e)(1) and (2) of the regulations. Membership in a non-profit "Indian" organization does not meet the definition of Indian under the Act and in section 309.2 of the regulations. Furthermore, if an "Indian spiritual leader" or tribal member adopts an individual, this action does not mean that the adopted individual is a member of a state or Federally-recognized tribe or is certified as an Indian artisan by a state or Federally-recognized tribe.

Definition of Indian Artisan, Section 309.2(b)

Several respondents suggested that the definition of Indian artisan should be clarified to read "an individual who is certified by an Indian tribe as its non-member artisan." This clarification has been adopted with a minor modification.

Definition of Indian Arts and Crafts Organization, Section 309.2(c)

Two respondents asked whether section 309.2(c) operates to exclude marketing entities, other than Indian arts and crafts organizations, from the law and regulations. Several others asserted that the definition of Indian arts and crafts organization should include any organization set up under tribal law, custom or authority, as well as under any other legal authority.

The Act broadly applies to the marketing of arts and crafts by any person in the United States. The reference to Indian arts and crafts organization as a protected group is not intended to suggest that the Act's regulation does not apply to all marketing activities. In addition, the Act's requirement that an Indian arts and crafts organization be legally established in order to meet the definition includes tribal law.

Definition of Indian Product, Section 309.2(d)

Several comments stated that the definition of Indian product should be more inclusive. One comment stated that the definition should be broad enough to include the work of musicians, actors, and writers. Another stated it should include all products made by an Indian. Several other comments stated that the definition of Indian product should also cover any cultural property of an Indian tribe or moiety and include a reference to a compatible Indian cultural property law. Still another respondent asserted that the proposed regulations incorrectly focus on "what good is made, not who made the good."

The final regulations do not adopt these comments. In keeping with the Indian Arts and Crafts Board's organic legislation, its primary mission, and the Congressional intent of the Act, the Board has determined in the final regulations that the Act applies to Indian arts and crafts and not to all products generally. However, what constitutes an Indian art or craft product is potentially very broad.

Several comments asked that the words "or produced" follow "made" in the definition of Indian product to underscore that art or craft is to be broadly construed.

Within the meaning of the statute, Indian arts and crafts mean any art or craft made by an Indian or Indian artisan. As the addition of the words "or produced" does not significantly enhance the definition of Indian product, the final regulations do not adopt this comment.

Several respondents stated that the 1935 cut off date for products regulated by the Act is arbitrary and should be dropped.

The final regulations do not adopt this comment. The focus on the contemporary arts and crafts market is in keeping with the Congressional intent of the Act and the legislated mission of the Indian Arts and Crafts Board—economic growth through the development and promotion of contemporary Indian arts and crafts.

Two comments asked that proposed section 309.2(d)(ii) be dropped so as to exclude from regulation by the Act products of a non-traditional Indian style or non-traditional Indian medium. Another comment asked that proposed section 309.2(d)(iii) include a reference to the difference between handmade, hand painted, and manufactured.

The final regulations do not adopt these comments. The proposed exclusion of products made in a non-traditional Indian style or non-traditional Indian medium runs counter to the legislative history of the Act, as the sponsors of the legislation were clearly aware of the evolution of such non-traditional products. The proposed exclusion is also inconsistent with a primary mission of the agency charged with carrying out the Act—the promotion of contemporary Indian arts and crafts. On the issue of production terms, handcrafts are clearly defined and anything else is not a handcraft. Additional descriptions in this section would make the regulations more complicated, and would not measurably improve the purpose of the regulations which is to define the nature and Indian origin of products covered by the Act.

One respondent supported the exclusion of industrial products from the proposed regulations, section 309.2(d)(2). Another asked that the products under this section be further clarified. Other respondents described the industrial products section as unclear and asked that it be removed. Upon further review, the exclusion for industrial products has been dropped from the final regulations because the provisions limiting the reach of the

Act to arts and crafts already exclude such products.

Another comment suggested that the regulations incorporate seven "classes" of products, based on the degree of Indianness of the maker and whether the product is a replica or import. The final regulations do not adopt the proposed classes of goods as they would make the regulations greatly more complicated and burdensome, and would not measurably improve the main purpose of the regulations which is to define rather than to classify the nature and Indian origin of products covered by the Act.

In final form, section 309.2(d) has been mildly reorganized and renumbered to improve readability.

Definition of Indian Tribe. Section 309.2(e)

One comment asked that all references in the regulations to "Indian tribe", the statutory term drawn from the Act, be revised to read "any federally-recognized tribes(s)", in recognition of consolidated tribes. This comment has not been adopted, as the definition of "Indian tribe" is provided in the Act, and the regulations cannot change the Act. However, all Federally-recognized consolidated tribes are, in fact, included in that definition.

One respondent asked that section 309.2(e)(2) include a provision to require state governments to use the same comprehensive tribal recognition criteria the Federal government uses for Federal recognition. This comment asserted that comprehensive procedures must be mandatory to prevent undermining the Act and those it is intended to protect. The final regulations do not require the use of comprehensive criteria for state recognition of tribes, as this goes beyond the authority of the Federal statute and is a matter of state authority. Additionally, the regulations do not set criteria for state tribal enrollment, as this is beyond the authority of the Federal statute.

Some comments asked for the addition of language in the regulations to include terminated California Indians and "federally-accepted tribal-preemption principles." Another asked that the Act protect all terminated tribes. These comments are not adopted into the final regulations. The regulations cannot change the Act, which makes no provision for terminated tribes.

Definition of Product of a Particular Indian Tribe or Indian Arts and Crafts Organization, Section 309.2(f)

One comment suggested the addition of the term "legally recognized Indian tribe" would help clarify the text of section 309.2(f). Another comment recommended the section include language for oversight of Indian tribes and arts and craft organizations.

These comments are not adopted into the final regulations. The term Indian tribe is defined earlier, in section 309.2(e), and the intent of this section is clear—to simply define the product of a particular Indian tribe or Indian arts and crafts organization.

Section 309.3
Interpretation of Statements About Indian Origin of Art or Craft Products

The final regulations clarify that the term "Indian" as used under the Act includes its market synonym "Native American."

One respondent stated that the regulations should work to prevent deceptive advertisements that use the name of a tribe to market a product, when the product is not made by a member of that tribe. Concern also was expressed about the use of phrases that refer to the "style" of a particular Indian tribe when the items are not made by artisans of that tribe, but imitate the work of that tribe. The respondent believed that the names of tribes as either nouns or adjectives should be for the exclusive use of the members of those tribes.

The Act and section 309.1 of the proposed regulations specifically state that it is unlawful to offer or display for sale or sell any good in a manner that falsely suggests it is the product of a particular Indian or Indian tribe or Indian arts and crafts organization. Section 309.3(a) also regulates the use of the unqualified name of an Indian tribe, and the unqualified term Indian, in connection with an art or craft product.

However, the use of a tribal name in conjunction with the word "style" is not prohibited by the Act or the regulations, as it is not necessarily misleading. The rights of tribes to control the use of their names, qualified and unqualified, is an issue of cultural patrimony and is beyond the scope of these regulations.

Several responses dealt with the issue of foreign products. Two respondents expressed concern over their perception of the undermining of permanent country-of-origin markings by importers of imitation Indian arts and crafts. One respondent expressed concern about foreign merchandise falsely marketed as "South American Indian" while another questioned the need of businesses to differentiate between products made by members of tribes resident in the United States and by members of foreign tribes.

The topic of permanent country-of-origin marking is beyond the scope of the Act and regulations. Under the Omnibus Trade Bill, Public Law 100-418, the U.S. Customs Service published regulations and oversees the requirement for permanent country-of-origin marking on imported Indian-style jewelry and other arts and crafts (19 CFR 134.43 (c)–(d).

Although the concern about products falsely marketed as South American Indian is beyond the scope of the regulations, identification of products of foreign Indian tribes is covered in section 309.3(b). The regulations require that products marketed in the United States must clearly show the name of the foreign country of the producer's tribal ancestry if the name of a tribe is used.

Section 309.4
Certification of Indian Artisans

One respondent expressed concern that the proposed regulations do not offer a "designation" for descendants that are not tribal members. A second expressed concern for individuals who are raised on reservations, but who are not tribal members because they do not meet tribal blood quantum requirements.

The Act adopts tribal certification as the exclusive approach to these situations, and the regulations simply carry out this Congressional mandate. Truthful statements may be made about Indian or tribal ancestry.

A number of comments supported the proposed regulations' measure of flexibility in the certification process and the placement of responsibility for the determination of individual cases upon an appropriate tribal authority.

Other respondents stated that the provision for tribal certification of Indian artisans under the proposed regulations should be clarified. The majority of these respondents were concerned that section 309.4 as proposed could allow a tribe to certify a person as an Indian artisan who is in no way connected with the tribe and who is not even of Indian ancestry. Those respondents maintained that the statute and its legislative history support the conclusion that Congress intended that Indian tribes should be able to certify persons as Indian artisans only if those persons were, first, of Indian ancestry and, second, of Indian ancestry connected with the certifying tribe. One response further suggested that to be eligible for certification one must prove lineal descent from a tribal member.

The final regulations adopt most of these comments. As amended, section 309.4 clarifies that to be eligible for certification as an Indian artisan by a particular tribe, the individual must be of the Indian ancestry of that tribe. The final regulations clarify that the certification must be documented in writing by the governing body of an Indian tribe or by a certifying body delegated this function by the governing body of an Indian tribe. The certification to be provided by the Indian tribe is that the individual is a non-member Indian artisan of the tribe.

Other comments asked that the regulations give Indian tribes guidance on procedures for the certification of Indian artists, such as documentation. In particular, one comment asked that the regulations also specify who within the tribe will have authority to make the certification decisions. One comment stated that procedural guidance would help prevent misuse of authority. Another stated it would encourage tribes to adopt certification programs. Others cautioned that care should be taken to avoid intrusion on tribal sovereignty.

While the final regulations clarify the overall requirements for certification, in deference to tribal sovereignty the actual certification procedures are left to the discretion of tribal governments.

One respondent expressed concern for individuals of various degrees of Indian ancestry, who are not tribal members, whose requests for Indian artisan certification are denied by the tribe. The respondent suggested that recognition of an individual's Indian ancestry by a state legislature should be an alternative to tribal certification. Another respondent suggested that recognition of an individual's Indian ancestry by a local entity, other than a tribe, should be sufficient for certification. These alternatives to tribal certification are not valid under the Act and are beyond the scope of the regulations. Truthful statements may be made about Indian or tribal heritage.

Finally, one respondent asked what specific authority prohibits the tribes from charging a fee for certification. The prohibition appears in section 107 of the Act (see also 25 U.S.C. 305e note).

Section 309.5 Penalties.

No comments received. However, language has been added to clarify what actions may subject a person to civil and criminal penalties.

Section 309.6 Complaints.

No comments received.

Drafting Information

These final regulations were prepared by Meridith Z. Stanton (Deputy Director, Indian Arts and Crafts Board) and Geoffrey E. Stamm (Director, Indian Arts and Crafts Board).

Compliance With Other Laws

This rule was not subject to Office of Management and Budget review under E.O. 12866.

There is no collection of information in this rule requiring approval by the Officer of Management and Budget under 44 U.S.C. 3504.

The Department of the Interior certifies that this rule will not have a significant economic effect on a substantial number of small entities under the Regulatory Flexibility Act (5 U. S. C. 601 et seq.). An unknown number of individuals, small businesses, and tribal governments may be affected in some way. These possible effects, such as increased demand on tribal governments from some of their members to document their status, stem from the statute itself rather than the regulations, as the preponderance of the regulations merely reflect statutory terms and requirements.

The Department of the Interior determined that these regulations will not have a significant effect on the human environment under the National Environmental Policy Act (42 U.S.C. 4321–4347). In addition, the Department of the Interior determined that these regulations are categorically excluded from the procedural requirements of the National Environmental Policy Act by Departmental regulations in 516 DM2. As such, there is no need for an Environmental Assessment or an Environmental Impact Statement.

List of Subjects in 25 CFR Part 309

Indians—Arts and crafts, Penalties.

For the reasons set out in the preamble, 25 CFR Chapter II is amended to add part 309 as follows:

PART 309—PROTECTION OF INDIAN ARTS AND CRAFTS PRODUCTS

Sec.

309.1 How do the regulations in this part carry out the Indian Arts and Crafts Act of 1990?

309.2 What are the key definitions for purposes of the Act?

309.3 How will statements about Indian origin of art or craft products be interpreted?

309.4 How can an individual be certified as an Indian artisan?

309.5 What penalties apply?
309.6 How are complaints filed?

Authority: 18 U. S. C. 1159, 25 U. S. C. 305 *et seq.*

§ 309.1 How do the regulations in this part carry out the Indian Arts and Crafts Act of 1990?

These regulations define the nature and Indian origin of products protected by the Indian Arts and Crafts Act of 1990 (18 U.S.C. 1159, 25 U.S.C. 305 et seq.) from false representations, and specify how the Indian Arts and Crafts Board will interpret certain conduct for enforcement purposes. The Act makes it unlawful to offer or display for sale or sell any good in a manner that falsely suggests it is Indian produced, an Indian product, or the product of a particular Indian, or Indian tribe, or Indian arts and crafts organization resident within the United States.

§ 309.2 What are the key definitions for purposes of the Act?

(a) *Indian* as applied to an individual means a person who is a member of an Indian tribe or for purposes of this part is certified by an Indian tribe as a non-member Indian artisan (in accordance with the provisions of § 309.4).

(b) *Indian artisan* means an individual who is certified by an Indian tribe as a non-member Indian artisan.

(c) *Indian arts and crafts organization* means any legally established arts and crafts marketing organization composed of members of Indian tribes.

(d) *Indian product.* (1) *In general,* Indian product means any art or craft product made by an Indian.

(2) *Illustrations.* The term "Indian product" includes, but is not limited to :

(i) Art works that are in a traditional or non-traditional Indian style or medium;

(ii) Crafts that are in a traditional or non-traditional Indian style or medium;

(iii) Handcrafts, i.e. objects created with the help of only such devices as allow the manual skill of the maker to condition the shape and design of each individual product.

(3) *Exclusion for products made before 1935.* The provisions of this part shall not apply to any art or craft products made before 1935.

(e) *Indian tribe* means—

(1) Any Indian tribe, band, nation, Alaska Native village, or any organized group or community which is recognized as eligible for the special programs and services provided by the United States to Indians because of their status as Indians; or

(2) Any Indian group that has been formally recognized as an Indian tribe by a State legislature or by a State commission or similar organization legislatively vested with State tribal recognition authority.

(f) *Product of a particular Indian tribe or Indian arts and crafts organization* means that the origin of a product is identified as a named Indian tribe or named Indian arts and crafts organization.

§ 309.3 How will statements about Indian origin of art or craft products be interpreted?

(a) *In general.* The unqualified use of the term "Indian" or of the term "Native American" or the unqualified use of the name of an Indian tribe, in connection with an art or craft product, is interpreted to mean for purposes of this part that—

(1) The maker is a member of an Indian tribe, is certified by an Indian tribe as a non-member Indian artisan, or is a member of the particular Indian tribe named; and

(2) The art or craft product is an Indian product.

(b) *Products of Indians of foreign tribes.* (1) *In general.* The unqualified use of the term "Indian" or of the term "Native American" or the unqualified use of the name of a foreign tribe, in connection with an art or craft product, regardless of where it is produced and regardless of any country-of-origin marking on the product, is interpreted to mean for purposes of this part that—

(i) The maker is a member of an Indian tribe, is certified by an Indian tribe as a non-member Indian artisan, or is a member of the particular Indian tribe named;

(ii) The tribe is resident in the United States; and

(iii) The art or craft product is an Indian product.

(2) *Exception where country of origin is disclosed.* Paragraph (b) of this section does not apply to any art or craft for which the name of the foreign country of tribal ancestry is clearly disclosed in conjunction with marketing of the product.

(c) *Example.* X is a lineal descendant of a member of Indian Tribe A. However, X is not a member of Indian Tribe A, nor is X certified by Indian Tribe A as a non-member Indian artisan. X may not be described in connection with the marketing of an art or craft product made by X as an Indian, a Native American, a member of an Indian tribe, a member of Tribe A, or as a non-member Indian artisan of an Indian tribe. However, the true statement may be used that X is of Indian descent, Native American descent, or Tribe A descent.

§ 309.4 How can an individual be certified as an Indian artisan?

(a) In order for an individual to be certified by an Indian tribe as a non-member Indian artisan for purposes of this part—

(1) The individual must be of Indian lineage of one or more members of such Indian tribe; and

(2) The certification must be documented in writing by the governing body of an Indian tribe or by a certifying body delegated this function by the governing body of the Indian tribe.

(b) As provided in section 107 of the Indian Arts and Crafts Act of 1990, Public Law 101-644, a tribe may not impose a fee for certifying an Indian artisan.

§ 309.5 What penalties apply?

A person who offers or displays for sale or sells a good, with or without a Government trademark, in a manner that falsely suggests it is Indian produced, an Indian product, or the product of a particular Indian or Indian tribe or Indian arts and crafts organization, resident within the United States:

(a) Is subject to the criminal penalties specified in section 1159, title 18, United States Code; and

(b) Is subject to the civil penalties specified in section 305e, title 25, United States Code.

§ 309.6
How are complaints filed?

Complaints about protected products alleged to be offered or displayed for sale or sold in a manner that falsely suggests they are Indian products should be made in writing and addressed to the Director, Indian Arts and Crafts Board, Room 4004-MIB, U.S. Department of the Interior, 1849 C Street, NW, Washington, DC 20240.

Dated: October 15, 1996.

NOTES

Introduction

1. Atlatl, based in Phoenix, Arizona, has a mission to "promote the vitality of Native American art." It does this by, among other things, providing an information network between Indian artists, art organizations, and other organizations; maintaining a registry of artists; sponsoring traveling art exhibitions; and providing workshops, consulting services, and technical assistance.

Chapter 1

1. Rennard Strickland says that *katcina* is the preferred spelling among many Pueblo peoples (1992: 183 n. 26). I have left the alternative spelling *kachina* in quotations from the written transcript.

Chapter 2

1. In 1824, the Bureau of Indian Affairs was created by the secretary of war as an agency of the War Department. It shortly thereafter became known as the Office of Indian Affairs. In 1834, the Bureau of Indian Affairs was created statutorily by Congress, and, in 1849, moved to the Department of the Interior (Kvasnicka 1988: 198).

Chapter 3

1. Joe Quetone to the author, Tallahassee, Fla., 18 April 1996. Quetone is the executive director of the Governor's Council on Indian Affairs.

2. Elaine Eff to the author, Crownsville, Md., 2 August 1993 and 8 April 1996. Eff is the acting administrator of the Maryland Conservation Program.

3. The information concerning state-recognized tribes, except where otherwise cited, was obtained through personal correspondence with the Indian Commission or governor's office in each state. The information has not been independently verified. I believe mine to be the only published compilation of these data for all state-recognized tribes.

4. Jane L. Weeks to the author, Montgomery, Ala., 28 July 1993; Eloise Josey to the author, Montgomery, Ala., 1996. Weeks was the executive director of the Alabama Indian Affairs Commission; Josey is the office manager for the Alabama Indian Affairs Commission.

5. Ed Sarabia to the author, Hartford, Conn., 6 August 1993 and 23 May 1996. Sarabia is the Indian Affairs coordinator for the State of Connecticut.

6. Byron H. Short to the author, 1993; Lynn Riley to the author, Dover, Del., 10 April 1996. Short worked for the Office of the Governor of Delaware; Riley is an executive assistant at the Division of Historical and Cultural Affairs, Department of State, State of Delaware.

7. Cyd H. Powell to the author, Atlanta, Ga., 2 August 1993; Billy Townsend to the author, Atlanta, Ga., 1 April 1996. Powell worked for the Office of the Governor of Georgia; Townsend is the chief historian of Georgia's state parks.

8. Diana Williamson to the author, Baton Rouge, La., 23 July 1993. Williamson was the executive director of the Louisiana Office of Indian Affairs.

9. John Peters to the author, Boston, Mass., 1993. Peters is the executive director of the Indian Affaris Council, State of Massachusetts.

10. John Peters, telephone call to the author, 11 June 1996.

11. Bruce A. Jones to the author, Raleigh, N.C., 22 July 1993; Gregory A. Richardson to the author, Raleigh, 8 April 1996. Jones is the executive director of the North Carolina Department

of Administration; Richardson is the director of the Indian Affairs Commission, State of North Carolina.

12. Robert C. Batson to the author, Albany, N.Y., 21 July 1993. Batson is a counsel for the Office of the Governor of New York.

13. Luvenia Butler to the author, Nashville, Tenn., 11 August 1993. Butler is the director of the Tennessee Commission on Indian Affairs.

14. Butler to the author, 1993, and 2 April 1996.

CHAPTER 4

1. The concept of "civil inattention" is from Irving Goffman's *Behavior in Public Places* (1963).

CHAPTER 5

1. Wilma P. Mankiller to Edwin Edwards, governor, State of Louisiana, 4 January 1992.

2. This account was pieced together from several primary and secondary sources, including newspaper articles. It has not been verified by the Cherokee Nation itself; I was unable to obtain an interview with a Cherokee tribal official in order to do so.

3. Thomas Jefferson Center to the author, Charlottesville, Va., 2 August 1993.

BIBLIOGRAPHY

Government Documents

Bingaman, Jeff. 1991. Senator Bingaman of New Mexico speaking on the Indian Arts and Crafts Act of 1990. 102nd Cong., 1st sess., *Cong. Rec.*, 26 November, vol. 137, pt. I, nos. S18150–3.

Florida Governor's Council on Indian Affairs, Inc. 1988. Policy Statement 88–1, 16 December.

Institute for Government Research. 1928. *The Problem of Indian Administration*, Lewis Meriam, technical director. The Brookings Institution. Baltimore, Maryland: The Lord Baltimore Press.

U.S. Bureau of the Census. 1990. *U.S. Census of Population: General Population Characteristics, United States*. U.S. Department of Commerce, Economics and Statistics Administration. Washington, D.C.

U.S. Commission on Civil Rights. 1981. *Indian Tribes: A Continuing Quest for Survival*. A Report of the United States Commission on Civil Rights. Washington, D.C.

U.S. Department of Commerce. 1985. "Study of Problems and Possible Remedies Concerning Imported Native American-Style Jewelry and Handicrafts." Automotive Affairs and Consumer Goods, International Trade Administration, report to the Congress.

U.S. Department of the Interior. 1991. *Summary and Text of Title 1: Public Law 101–644*. Indian Arts and Crafts Board.

———. 1991–93. American Indian Arts and Crafts Board. Files: Letters and Written Statements.

———. 1993. "Types of Products Affected by Pub. L. 101–644, the Indian Arts and Crafts Act of 1990." Memorandum, Solicitor-Indian Affairs, 23 April.

———. 1995. "Terminated Tribes Restored to Federal Status." Bureau of Indian Affairs, Branch of Tribal Relations, 23 January.

———. 1996. "Summary Statement of Acknowledgment Cases." Bureau of Indian Affairs, Branch of Acknowledgment and Research, 22 March.

U.S. House. 1989a. Committee on Interior and Insular Affairs. *To Expand the Powers of the Indian Arts and Crafts Board*. 101st Cong., 1st sess., 17 August.

———. 1989b. Committee on Interior and Insular Affairs. *To Provide Federal Recognition for the Lumbee Tribe of North Carolina*. 101st Cong., 1st sess., 26 September.

U.S. Senate. 1991a. Select Committee on Indian Affairs. *To Transfer Administrative Consideration of Applications for Federal Recognition of an Indian Tribe to an Independent Commission*. 102nd Cong., 1st sess., 22 October.

———. 1991b. Select Committee on Indian Affairs. *Providing for the Recognition of the Lumbee Tribe of Cheraw Indians of North Carolina, and for Other Purposes*. 102nd Cong., 1st sess., 26 November.

Books and Articles

Anders, Gary C. 1992. "A Critical Analysis of the Alaska Native Claims and Native Corporate Development." In *Native Americans and Public Policy,* edited by Fremont J. Lyden and Lyman H. Legters, 85–112. Pittsburgh: University of Pittsburgh Press.

Atchison, Sandra D. 1988. "Who Is an Indian, and Why Are They Asking?" *Business Week,* 26 December, 71.

Barron, Jerome A., and C. Thomas Dienes. 1991. *Constitutional Law in a Nutshell*. 2nd ed. St. Paul, Minn.: West Publishing Company.

Barsh, Russel Lawrence, and James Youngblood Henderson. 1980. *The Road: Indian Tribes and Political Liberty*. Berkeley: University of California Press.

Barth, Fredrik. 1969. *Ethnic Groups and Boundaries: The Social Organization of Culture Difference*. London: George Allen & Unwin.

Beale, Calvin L. 1972. "An Overview of the Phenomenon of Mixed Racial Isolates in the United States." *American Anthropologist* 74 (3): 704–710.

Becker, Howard S. 1982. *Art Worlds*. Berkeley: University of California Press.

Black, Henry Campbell. 1968. *Black's Law Dictionary: Definitions of the Terms and Phrases of American and English Jurisprudence, Ancient and Modern*. 4th ed. St. Paul, Minn.: West Publishing Company.

Blackwell, Charles W., and J. Patrick Mehaffey. 1983. "American Indians, Trust and Recognition." In *Nonrecognized American Indian Tribes: An Historical and Legal Perspective*, edited by Frank W. Porter, III, 50–73. Occasional Papers Series no. 7. Chicago: The Newberry Library Center for the History of the American Indian.

Blu, Karen I. 1980. *The Lumbee Problem: The Making of an American Indian People*. Cambridge: Cambridge University Press.

Brody, J. J. 1976. "The Creative Consumer: Survival, Revival and Invention in Southwest Indian Arts." In *Ethnic and Tourist Arts*, edited by Nelson H. H. Graburn, 70–84. Berkeley: University of California Press.

Burman, Sandra B., and Barbara Harrell-Bond, eds. 1979. *The Imposition of Law*. New York: Academic Press.

Burton, Lloyd. 1991. *American Indian Water Rights and the Limits of Law*. Lawrence: University Press of Kansas.

Campbell, Ben Nighthorse. 1991. Letter to the editor. *The Indian Trader*, 4 September.

Campisi, Jack. 1991. *The Mashpee Indians: Tribe on Trial.* Syracuse: Syracuse University Press.

Canby, William C., Jr. 1988. *American Indian Law in a Nutshell.* 2nd ed. St. Paul, Minn.: West Publishing Company.

Christian, Timothy. 1989. Introduction to *The Law of Nations and the New World,* by L. C. Green and Olive P. Dickason. Edmonton: University of Alberta Press.

Cohen, Felix S. 1982. *Felix S. Cohen's Handbook of Federal Indian Law,* rev. ed., edited by Rennard Strickland, et al. Charlottesville, Va.: Michie Bobbs Merrill.

Collier, Jane F. 1993. "Nationalism and Studies of Law." *Political and Legal Anthropology Review* 16 (3): 1–7.

Colson, Elizabeth. 1953. *The Makah Indians.* Minneapolis: University of Minnesota Press.

Coombe, Rosemary J. 1989. "Objects of Property and Subjects of Politics: Intellectual Property Laws and Democratic Dialogue." *Texas Law Review* 69 (7): 1853–80.

Dane, J. K., and Eugene Griessman. 1972. "The Collective Identity of Marginal Peoples: The North Carolina Experience." *American Anthropologist* 74 (3): 694–704.

Debo, Angie. 1940. *And Still the Waters Run: The Betrayal of the Five Civilized Tribes.* Princeton, N.J.: Princeton University Press.

Deloria, Vine, Jr. 1974. *Behind the Trail of Broken Treaties: An Indian Declaration of Independence.* New York: Delacorte.

———. 1985. "The Evolution of Federal Indian Policy Making." In *American Indian Policy in the Twentieth Century,* edited by Vine Deloria, Jr., 239–56. Norman: University of Oklahoma Press.

Deloria, Vine, Jr., and Clifford Lytle. 1984. *The Nations Within: The Past and Future of American Indian Sovereignty.* New York: Pantheon Books.

Dockstader, Frederick J. 1961. *Indian Art in America.* London: Studio Books.

Esber, George S. 1992. "Shortcomings of the Indian Self-Determination Policy." In *State and Reservation: New*

Perspectives on Federal Indian Policy, edited by George Pierre Castile and Robert L. Bee, 212–23. Tucson: University of Arizona Press.

Evans-Pritchard, E. E. 1940. *The Nuer: A Description of the Modes of Livelihood and Political Institutions of a Nilotic People.* Oxford: Oxford University Press.

Falkowski, James E. 1992. *Indian Law/Race Law: A Five-Hundred Year History.* New York: Praeger.

Felcher, Peter L., and Edward L. Rubin. 1980. "The Descendibility of the Right of Publicity: Is There Commercial Life after Death?" *Yale Law Journal* 89 (6): 1125–32.

Fost, Dan. 1991. "American Indians in the 1990s." *American Demographics* 13 (December): 26–34.

Fried, Morton H. 1968. "On the Concepts of 'Tribe' and 'Tribal Society.'" In *Essays on the Problem of Tribe,* edited by June Helm, 3–20. Proceedings of the 1967 Annual Spring Meeting of the American Ethnological Society. Seattle: University of Washington Press.

Gearing, Fred. 1968. "Sovereignties and Jural Communities in Political Evolution." In *Essays on the Problem of Tribe,* edited by June Helm, 111–19. Proceedings of the 1967 Annual Spring Meeting of the American Ethnological Society. Seattle: University of Washington Press.

Ghere, David L. 1993. "The 'Disappearance' of the Abenaki in Western Maine: Political Organization and Ethnocentric Assumptions." *American Indian Quarterly* 17 (2): 193–207.

Goffman, Irving. 1963. *Behavior in Public Places.* New York: Free Press.

Graburn, Nelson, H. H., ed. 1976. *Ethnic and Tourist Arts: Cultural Expressions from the Fourth World.* Berkeley: University of California Press.

Green, L. C., and Olive P. Dickason. 1976. *The Law of Nations and the New World.* Edmonton: The University of Alberta Press.

Green, Rayna. 1988. "The Tribe Called Wannabee." *Folklore* 99 (i): 30–55.

Greenbaum, Susan. 1991. "What's in a Label? Identity Problems of Southern Indian Tribes." *The Journal of Ethnic Studies* 19 (Summer): 107–26.

Griessman, B. Eugene. 1972. "The American Isolates." *American Anthropologist* 74 (3): 693–94.

Grossman, George S. 1979. *The Sovereignty of American Indian Tribes: A Matter of Legal History.* Minneapolis: Minnesota Civil Liberties Union Foundation.

———. 1988. "Indians and the Law." In *New Directions in American Indian History,* edited by Colin G. Calloway, 97–126. Norman: University of Oklahoma Press.

Hales, Donna. 1990a. "Tribe Touts Unregistered Artists." *Muskogee (Okla.) Daily Phoenix,* 3 September, 1A, 10A.

———. 1990b. "Selling Bogus Indian Art Is Illegal." *Muskogee (Okla.) Daily Phoenix,* 3 September, 3A.

Harjo, Suzan S. 1991. "Legislation Stiffens Art Authenticity Laws." *Lakota (S.Dak.) Times,* 11 September, A6.

Jacobson-Widding, Anita. 1983. *Identity: Personal and Socio-Cultural.* Acta University Uppsala, Uppsala Studies in Cultural Anthropology 5. Atlantic Highlands, N.J.: Humanities Press.

Kickingbird, Kirke, and Karen Ducheneaux. 1973. *One Hundred Million Acres.* New York: Macmillan.

Kidder, Robert L. 1979. "Toward an Integrated Theory of Imposed Law." In *The Imposition of Law,* edited by Sandra B. Burman and Barbara Harrell-Bond, 289–305. New York: Academic Press.

Kvasnicka, Robert M. 1988. "United States Indian Treaties and Agreements." In *History of Indian-White Relations,* edited by Wilcomb E. Washburn, 195–201. Vol. 4, *Handbook of North American Indians,* gen. ed. William C. Sturtevant. Washington, D.C.: Smithsonian Institution.

Lange, David. 1981. "Recognizing the Public Domain." *Law and Contemporary Problems* 44 (4): 147–78.

Lerch, Patricia Barker. 1992. "State-Recognized Indians of North Carolina, Including a History of the Waccamaw Sioux."

In *Indians of the Southeastern United States in the Late 20th Century,* edited by J. Anthony Paredes, 44–71. Tuscaloosa: University of Alabama Press.

Longfish, George C., and Joan Randall. 1988. "Contemporary Native American Art: Contradictions in Indian Territory." *Journal of Arts Management and Law* 18 (2): 20–24.

Lyden, Fremont J., and Lyman H. Legters, eds. 1992. *Native Americans and Public Policy.* Pittsburgh: University of Pittsburgh Press.

Mankiller, Wilma. 1990. "Buyers Have Final Say on Indian Art." *Muskogee (Okla.) Daily Phoenix,* 21 December, 7A.

McAlester (Okla.) News-Capital & Democrat. 1990. "Congress' Help Hurts Indians." 21 December, 1A.

McCready, William C. 1983. *Culture, Ethnicity, and Identity: Current Issues in Research.* New York: Academic Press.

McGuire, Thomas R. 1990. "Federal Indian Policy: A Framework for Evaluation." *Human Organization* 49 (3): 206–16.

McSweeney, Karen. 1993. "The Indian Arts and Crafts Act of 1990." In *Sovereignty Symposium VI: The Word of the People.* Symposium, Tulsa, Okla., 8–10 June. The Oklahoma Supreme Court, The Oklahoma Indian Affairs Commission & The Sovereignty Symposium, Inc., sec. 10.

Morris, C. Patrick. 1992. "Termination by Accountants: The Reagan Indian Policy." In *Native Americans and Public Policy,* edited by Fremont J. Lyden and Lyman H. Legters, 63–84. Pittsburgh: University of Pittsburgh Press.

Nader, Laura. 1988. "Up the Anthropologist—Perspectives Gained from Studying Up." In *Anthropology for the Nineties,* edited by Johnnetta B. Cole, 470–84. New York: Collier.

Nagel, Joane. 1996. *American Indian Ethnic Renewal: Red Power and the Resurgence of Identity and Culture.* New York and London: Oxford University Press.

Olson, James S., and Raymond Wilson. 1984. *Native Americans in the Twentieth Century.* Provo: Brigham Young University Press.

Parks, Douglas R. 1988. "The Importance of Language Study for the Writing of Plains Indian History." In *New Directions in American Indian History*, edited by Colin G. Calloway, 153–97. Norman: University of Oklahoma Press.

Parsley, Jon Keith. 1993. "Regulation of Counterfeit Indian Arts and Crafts: An Analysis of the Indian Arts and Crafts Act of 1990." *American Indian Law Review* 18 (2): 487–514.

Porter, Frank W., III. 1983. "An Historical Perspective on Nonrecognized American Indian Tribes." In *Nonrecognized American Indian Tribes: An Historical and Legal Perspective*, edited by Frank W. Porter, III, 1–49. Newberry Library Occasional Papers, no. 7. Chicago: Newberry Library for the History of the American Indian.

Prucha, Francis Paul. 1994. *American Indian Treaties: The History of a Political Anomaly*. Berkeley: University of California Press.

Ragsdale, Fred L., Jr. 1985. "The Deception of Geography." In *American Indian Policy in the Twentieth Century*, edited by Vine Deloria, Jr., 63–82. Norman: University of Oklahoma Press.

Roosens, Eugeen E. 1989. *Creating Ethnicity: The Process of Ethnogenesis*. Newbury Park, Calif.: Sage Publications.

Rosen, Steven. 1993. "Airport 'Tribute' Art Project Takes Heat on Indian Entrants." *Denver (Colo.) Post*, 28 March, 5I.

Roth, George. 1992. "Overview of Southeastern Indian Tribes Today." In *Indians of the Southeastern United States in the Late 20th Century*, edited by J. Anthony Paredes, 183–202. Tuscaloosa: University of Alabama Press.

Rountree, Helen C. 1992. "Indian Virginians on the Move." In *Indians of the Southeastern United States in the Late 20th Century*, edited by J. Anthony Paredes, 9–28. Tuscaloosa: University of Alabama Press.

Royce, Anya Peterson. 1982. *Ethnic Identity: Strategies of Diversity*. Bloomington: Indiana University Press.

Schrader, Robert Fay. 1983. *The Indian Arts and Crafts Board: An Aspect of New Deal Indian Policy*. Albuquerque: University of New Mexico Press.

Service, Elman R. 1962. *Primitive Social Organization*. New York: Random House.

Sider, Gerald M. 1993. *Lumbee Indian Histories: Race, Ethnicity and Indian Identity in the Southern United States*. Cambridge: Cambridge University Press.

Simmons, James L. 1977. "One Little, Two Little, Three Little Indians: Counting American Indians in Urban Society." *Human Organization* 36 (1): 76–79.

Snipp, C. Matthew. 1989. *American Indians: The First of This Land*. New York: Russell Sage Foundation.

Snyder, Francis G. 1989. "Thinking about 'Interests': Legislative Process in the European Community." In *History and Power in the Study of the Law: New Directions in Legal Anthropology*, edited by June Starr and Jane F. Collier, 168–98. Ithaca, N.Y.: Cornell University Press.

Spicer, Edward H. 1971. "Persistent Cultural Systems." *Science* 174 (4011): 795–800.

Starr, June, and Jane F. Collier, eds. 1989. *History and Power in the Study of the Law: New Directions in Legal Anthropology*. Ithaca, N.Y.: Cornell University Press.

Steward, Julian. 1955. *Theory of Culture Change*. Urbana: University of Illinois Press.

Strickland, Rennard. 1992. "Implementing the National Policy of Understanding, Preserving, and Safeguarding the Heritage of Indian Peoples and Native Hawaiians: Human Rights, Sacred Objects, and Cultural Patrimony." *Arizona State Law Journal* 24 (1): 175–91.

Sturtevant, William C. 1983. "Tribe and State in the Sixteenth and Twentieth Centuries." In *The Development of Political Organization in Native America: 1979 Proceedings of the American Ethnological Society*, edited by Elisabeth Tooker, 3–16. Washington, D.C.: The American Ethnological Society.

Sunstein, Cass R. 1990. "Norms in Surprising Places: The Case of Statutory Interpretation." *Ethics* 100 (July): 803–20.

Svensson, Frances. 1979. "Imposed Law and the Manipulation of Identity: The American Indian Case." In *The Imposition of*

Law, edited by Sandra B. Burman and Barbara Harrell-Bond, 69–87. New York: Academic Press.

Thornton, Russell. 1987. *American Holocaust and Survival: A Population History since 1492*. Norman: University of Oklahoma Press.

———. 1990. *The Cherokees: A Population History*. Lincoln: University of Nebraska Press.

Toland, Judith D., ed. 1993. *Ethnicity and the State*. Political and Legal Anthropology, vol. 9. New Brunswick, N.J.: Transaction Publishers.

Trosper, Ronald. 1976. "Native American Boundary Maintenance: The Flathead Indian Reservation, Montana, 1869–1970." *Ethnicity* 3: 256–74.

Turner, Victor. 1974. *Dramas, Fields and Metaphors: Symbolic Action in Human Society*. Ithaca, N.Y.: Cornell University Press.

United Nations. 1993. "Conserving Heritage: Cultural and Intellectual Property Rights." *UN Chronicle* 30 (June): 50–51.

Unrau, William E. 1989. *Mixed Bloods and Tribal Dissolution: Charles Curtis and the Quest for Indian Identity*. Lawrence: University Press of Kansas.

Viola, Herman J. 1993. *Ben Nighthorse Campbell: An American Warrior*. New York: Orion Books.

Vizenor, Gerald. 1990. *Crossbloods: Bone Courts, Bingo and Other Reports*. Minneapolis: University Of Minnesota Press.

Weatherhead, L. R. 1980. "What is an 'Indian Tribe'?—The Question of Tribal Existence." *American Indian Law Review* 8 (1): 1–47.

Weibel-Orlando, Joan. 1991. *Indian Country, L.A.: Maintaining Ethnic Community in Complex Society*. Urbana: University of Illinois Press.

Wilkinson, Charles H. 1987. *American Indians, Time and the Law: Native Societies in a Modern Constitutional Society*. New Haven: Yale University Press.

———. 1992. *The Eagle Bird: Mapping a New West*. New York: Pantheon Books.

Winter, Steven. 1989. "Transcendental Nonsense, Metaphoric Reasoning, and the Cognitive Stakes for Law." *University of Pennsylvania Law Review* 137 (4): 1105–237.

NONWRITTEN SOURCES

Atlatl. 1992. Panel Discussion, Indian Arts and Crafts Act of 1990, at the Biennial Conference of Atlatl, a Native American Arts Service Organization, Minneapolis, Minn., October 22–25. Tape recording.

Public Forum on Indian Arts and Crafts Act of 1990, Oklahoma City, Okla., 15 January. Oklahoma Historical Society, Oral History Program Collection. Archives Division, Oklahoma City, Okla. Tape recording by Rodger Harris.

Sovereignty Symposium IV. 1991. Panel discussion, Indian Arts and Crafts Act of 1990, Oklahoma City, Okla., 11 June. Oklahoma Historical Society, Archives Division, Oklahoma City, Okla. Video recording (partial).

Thomas Jefferson Center for the Protection of Free Expression. 1993. Meeting sponsored by the Thomas Jefferson Center for the Protection of Free Expression, Charlottesville, Va., 22 June, held in U.S. Capitol, Washington, D.C.

INDEX